BOUNCE
&
THE OPPOSITE OF SEX

BOUNCE
&
THE OPPOSITE OF SEX
Don Roos

faber and faber

Bounce was first published in the United States in 2000 by
Talk Miramax Books/Hyperion
First published in the United Kingdom in 2001
by Faber and Faber Limited
3 Queen Square London WC1N 3AU

Bounce is published by arrangement with Hyperion, 77 w. 66th Street,
New York, New York 10023-6298

Photoset by Faber and Faber Ltd
Printed in England by Mackays of Chatham plc, Chatham, Kent

All rights reserved

© Don Roos, 2001
Photographs from *Bounce* by Eric Lee © 2000 Miramax Films
Photographs from *The Opposite of Sex* by Bob Akester © 2000 Sony
Pictures Classics

The right of Don Roos to be identified as author of this work has been asserted in
accordance with Section 77 of the Copyright, Designs and Patents Act 1998

*This book is sold subject to the condition that it shall not, by way of trade or
otherwise, be lent, resold, hired out or otherwise circulated without the publisher's
prior consent in any form of binding or cover other than that in which it is
published and without a similar condition including this condition being imposed
on the subsequent purchaser*

A CIP record for this book
is available from the British Library

ISBN 0-571-20921-1

2 4 6 8 10 9 7 5 3 1

CONTENTS

Introduction by Don Roos, vii

BOUNCE, 1
THE OPPOSITE OF SEX, 131

Don Roos

INTRODUCTION

In 1995, fourteen years after my first pay-cheque as a writer for the screen, I decided – more out of frustration than desire – that I had to direct my own scripts. It's not an uncommon ambition in Hollywood, where the writer is required to stand quietly on the sidelines as the director plays with all the toys and cuts lines.

Not that I subscribe to the popular notion that writers are the beaten-down, powerless, bottom-dwellers of the film industry. For one thing, we can write; we can start a movie right now, with a piece of paper and a pen; of all the unions in Hollywood, only the Writers Guild has a membership that can do its job without being hired. And while a director without a writer can do nothing and is thereby miserable, a writer without a director is as happy as he'll ever be.

Still, a director gets to talk to actors – and actors and their mysterious effect on us in the dark when we were young is the only reason any of us is in show business; and a director decides what the camera shows us of the scripts we've labored on; and a director receives a hundred times more flattery than criticism, which is the exact reverse of what a writer gets. So I wanted to direct, naturally, and I promised myself I'd treat the writer – who would, coincidentally, be myself – like a king.

I wrote a script, got a bankable female star to agree to be directed by me, and found a studio willing to hire me and pay her. Then in March 1996 occurred a disaster no less painful for being commonplace: the studio disliked what once they had liked, the bankable female star withdrew, and soon all that was left of the whole venture was a pair of matched lawsuits, later settled.

I wrote *The Opposite of Sex* in reaction to all that – and particularly to the rumor that the movie fell apart because my main character was 'unlikable'. Hollywood doesn't like unlikable characters, particularly women, and so in our movies the leading female character usually enters a room with a bag of groceries after struggling endearingly with the lock while the telephone rings all the while, and in her desperate struggle (it might be a date) to reach said phone trips on her cat (the friend of lonely, non-threatening, likable women), drops her bag of groceries, yelps as she tumbles to the floor, and lands ample chest down on a spilled carton of comically, charmingly exploded eggs. Plus she misses the call, naturally. Now *that's* likable. I'd had my fill of those heroines by March of 1996, and this time I swore I'd write a main female character so unlikable that no one could plausibly hope she'd emerge charming even after numerous and punishing rewrites. She'd be irredeemably offensive, and I couldn't wait.

It turns out I didn't have to. Dedee Truitt arrived in my head almost immediately with an image that still opens the movie: a teenage girl, old for her years, throwing a chair instead of a clod of earth into an open grave. The other characters evolved soon after that, and when it became clear that I was going to write about a gay man's love life, I knew Dedee would be required to be more than unlikable; she'd have to be disarming.

In the United States, though we do love our gay characters, particularly when they are the female star's best friends and drop by regularly to give makeovers and say, 'Men are pigs,' we don't like to think of their love lives all that much. As in, never. If I wanted to make this gay stuff palatable to my squeamish audience, I would have to put their opinions in Dedee's mouth. If she found it creepy, if she rolled her eyes, maybe the audience, feeling that its point of view was acknowledged, would relax. I don't like polemical films or politically correct films or anything where I can see the author standing behind the characters, whispering words into their ears. So Dedee became a little bit of a bigot – although for me she has the saving grace of finding everyone, not just a class or two, boring and disgusting – and by the end of the film, when she suffers homosexuality to exist, I was hoping my audience would follow her lead. I've always found a bigot saying something mildly liberal more convincing than a liberal saying almost anything.

Fired up now, and as grouchy as I'd ever been, I decided to break as many of the Rules of Screenwriting as I could that summer. Here are a few of the sacred cows I grilled, some of which will be familiar to anyone who's read any one of those *How to Write a Script* books:

1 Have a likable hero. (See above.)
2 Not so much talking, please. Words are counter-cinematic and

the sign of a bad writer. Hamlet's soliloquy could have all been done as a close-up, totally silent except perhaps for a little score using Danish woodwinds if they had them then, because everything else is just blah-blah-blah.

3 No ensembles, please. Star parts only. Easier to cast, easier to sell.
4 No flashbacks or flash-forwards or anything of that kind, if you don't mind. People are tired, they've got things to eat, they don't want to be jostled backwards and forwards through time.
5 And, it need hardly be said, no voice-over at all. Unless of course, you're adapting from a book, and then you can use one or two little voice-over speeches at the beginning and end of the movie as bookends, in the following manner:

EXT. SNOWY FIELD – DAY

Late afternoon. A farmhouse in the distance. A herd of cows heading towards the barn.

      NARRATOR (V.O.)
     (*as pensive and wistful as possible*)
 It was a late afternoon in winter, and the cows were heading towards the barn.

A young girl appears dragging a stick in the snowy fields, and therefore:

      NARRATOR (V.O.)
 I could often be found in the fields that winter, dragging a stick in the snow . . .

Can you blame me for wanting to do it differently?

Of course the biggest taboo was the one forbidding any real treatment of a gay man's love life. A leading character was never gay unless it was an absolutely necessary part of his story arc. He could be dying of AIDS (preferably in a courtroom), or coming out of the closet (preferably in a dress), but that was it. You just didn't talk about a man's desire for another man as you would a man's desire for a woman. All of that popcorn could come up as easily as it went down, after all. But I didn't care. I was off and running.

And I didn't throw out *all* convention. After all, Dedee is a bad-girl-stranger-in-town, not the most original character on God's earth, and just to keep the story familiar I threw in a gun, and a murder, and a blonde bimbo (who was actually brunette in this case and a guy), and a birth, and a happy ending, and I capped it off with a fairly conventional moral which, when you put it into words, is fairly embarrassing: that people, most people, are really more worth your while than not. And so, steering uneasily between conventionality and iconoclasm, I and the script progressed, and I have never felt as free before or since as I did while writing it.

Then it was finished and I was instantly ashamed. I felt as if I'd taken off all my clothes and paraded down Wilshire Boulevard. I sent it off to my agent and waited, not really thinking much would come of it, and almost hoping the whole thing would die quietly. (Its death would be hastened, I believed, by my demand to direct it.) In the meantime, I would repent with a straight romance: *Bounce*. Unlike *Opposite*, which required weeks of plotting and re-plotting, the idea for *Bounce* came almost full-blown into my mind on a Monday night; by that Friday I had an outline and thirty pages of script; and three weeks later it was finished in a rough state, then rewritten in three more.

Rebound was the theme of that year, because *Bounce* was very much a rebound reaction to *The Opposite of Sex*, as that was to the experience of the earlier, doomed movie. *Opposite*, for all its surface outrageousness, betrayed my eagerness to please on every page. If I felt I had to put some necessary exposition in, I would have my narrator say, 'Oh, this is dull, so let me give you the broad strokes of what happens here.' If I was concerned that some members of the audience would object to a man kissing another man, I used Dedee to laugh at them before they could laugh at me. I tried very hard to imply that if you, as an audience member, didn't respond the way I liked, it was because you were, well, unhip or corny or not worthy of notice. And it was fun, but I was also aware that it was cheating. I was a writer who cultivated his own deniability.

So in *Bounce* I wanted to do it the hard way: to tell my story plainly, without irony or winking at the audience, without characters offering disclaimers, to let the story and the characters sink or swim on their own merits. And I wanted it to be about straight people, because a love story about straight people can be felt by the gay audience (who is used to gender translation) and the straight audience alike. And I frankly wanted to see if I could tell a love story that interested me within the confines of a Hollywood movie, because while Hollywood makes dozens of romantic comedies, adult love stories are much more difficult. For me, the challenge was a big one: sincerity over irony; genuine feeling over laughter. And because this was a movie for movie stars, I never intended to direct it. What big stars would trust me? I just wanted to see if I could write it. And sell it, too, because I knew *Opposite* would go nowhere fast.

In fact, *Bounce* did sell very quickly, in days actually, and while the studio was finding a director and a cast, I began pre-production on *The Opposite of Sex* – because that, miraculously, did find a studio, one that was limping towards its sad end but a studio nonetheless. Cameras rolled in June of 1997 so I postponed a rewrite of *Bounce* and started to learn how to direct on the job.

How do I explain the feeling of finally directing my own work? I wasn't terrified, first of all. Part of me never believed it was actually going to happen, so I went into it in a haze of denial that cut a lot of the fear. And even when the first day arrived, when I actually had to say 'action' (which I tended to say too soon, before the camera had shifted focus from the clapperboard to the actors), it all felt so much easier, more natural than I anticipated. I had seen the movie in my head, and all I needed to do was rely on the people surrounding me, all of whom were there to make me look good. In many ways, directing is the opposite of writing. Directing is social; writing is not. Directing is interpreting or conducting; writing is creating, composing. And directing is fun, and you have your own trailer, and people treat you as if you know everything. Writers are treated as if they know typing, and you don't have a trailer, and it isn't fun, at least not for me. Still, writing's the better occupation – to be there in the beginning, to make something out of nothing. Yes, it's a much better occupation. Ask God. It's just a worse job.

Not to say that I didn't have problems directing. I didn't know a gaffer from a grip, and I'm not a spatial person, so the three-dimensionality of staging action was a challenge. And the hours are long, and they do overfeed you, and so by the end of the film you look considerably worse than you did at the beginning. And I hated my dailies and wouldn't watch them, a bad habit I maintain to this day.

But the actors were a joy. Finally to be allowed to speak to the people most responsible for bringing your characters to life was a heady new privilege. And what actors: Christina Ricci, Martin Donovan, Lisa Kudrow, Ivan Sergei, Lyle Lovett, Johnny Galecki . . . Very patient with me, very generous with their trust and affection. They were all much braver than I was – the women in particular. Christina refused to falsely ingratiate herself to the audience or to ask for its sympathy, and Lisa didn't care how we made her look as long as it was right for the character. Her hair was tortured into braids and buns and twists, and most of her outfits looked as if economy and comfort were her shopping bywords.

I was a good friend to the writer. There was no ad-libbing, and I would re-take a scene if a word was dropped that hurt the rhythm of a line. If a line wasn't immediately working I'd much rather have the actor work harder than the writer (who was directing and therefore very tired and probably not thinking as well as he was that day a year ago when he wrote the line). But inevitably there would be rewrites based on an actor's question or concern, because very soon, within their first week on the film, the actors begin to know the characters better or more deeply than the writer does. And Lisa Kudrow gave me one or two really funny lines which I'm hoping she's forgotten. But most of the rewriting took place during the editing process, when an actor's eyes or face or intonation suddenly made everything clear – and sometimes a whole scene redundant. We didn't include the school library scene, for example, in the film, though we shot it the first day. I don't miss it. Everything Lucia feels about Matt and Bill and Dedee she's already shown us in her face, or will soon.

The Opposite of Sex opened in May of 1998, and several weeks later I got a call from the studio which purchased *Bounce* suggesting that I direct it. The excitement I felt at this was instantly tempered somewhat when they said they couldn't get anyone else to do it. Still, it was an offer, and I accepted it gladly. A few months later Miramax acquired the package from this also-fatally-ill studio, and in the spring of 1999 I began pre-production.

Of course, by now I knew enough about directing to be terrified. And all the things I had wanted to do in *Bounce* when I thought some other director was going to have to make it work I bitterly regretted. Why hadn't I written a character who could apologize for the movie to its audience? But despite my misgivings we were off and running, and worse yet, not in a small way, because Miramax wanted to offer Ben Affleck and Gwyneth Paltrow the leads. I wanted them too, even though their Oscars intimidated me, so at the studio's request they met with me and agreed to do the movie.

I was worried that the experience of shooting *Bounce* would be tough after the wonderful time we had on *Opposite*. I shouldn't have been. It was a perfect production experience. We had a studio that loved movies (rare nowadays), we had more money, we had a wonderful producer who made each day magically seamless, *and* a dream crew, *and* a cast of such even-tempered, talented professionals that I'd happily shoot the whole thing over just to spend fifty twelve-hour days with them again. And to top it off, Gwyneth and Ben never once mentioned their Oscars when we were debating a line or a piece of blocking or business, although several times I believe I caught them thinking of their statuettes and smiling as I blathered.

There was another difference between the two films. *The Opposite of Sex* was a constructed movie. Even though the voice-over was written with the script, not until it was re-recorded and laid in, and the editing complete, did the movie emerge. Working on it, none of us quite had a handle on it. Would this play funny? Would this be sad? We couldn't answer any of those questions once we began that film.

But *Bounce* wasn't a constructed movie in that sense. It's a simple story, and it's easy for us, I think, to understand what the characters are going through. We've all told small lies that grow despite our attempts to stop them; we've all been nervous in airports; all of us can imagine a knock on the door that brings the end of our world; we all admire small braveries; we all fall in love, or wish to; we all feel betrayed by someone we love, or by ourselves. And so very quickly the movie's tone and theme and emotions had their effect on us. It's a movie about grief and loneliness, and family and love, and by the last day of shooting all of us, I think, felt that we'd gone through a special experience.

My favorite moment in production occurred one night in a diner on the outskirts of Los Angeles, where Gwyneth and Ben were playing a scene in the front seat of Abby's late husband's car, and she's telling him how she once had a baby in a car, almost, and he's falling in love with her as she talks, and they kiss at the end. And we did the scene easily a dozen times, and each time it was good and a little different, and each time, despite the walkie-talkies and the lights, and the dozens of people milling about, and the cars on the street beyond honking their horns to ruin the take, despite all the evidence of artificiality going on around us, I believed that these two people, saying lines I had written a year or more ago, were real, and I was an invisible witness to this private, almost too-intimate exchange. And I thought, 'What a privilege to be here.' That's the real joy of directing films over writing films: you are there on the spot when it all finally happens, when the words are said and the kisses or blows delivered, and suddenly it happens for you like you dreamed it would when you were a kid, sitting in a theater and wishing you were up there, in there, inside that world.

And that's a little how I feel about reading screenplays. I've learned a lot from reading them, studying them and comparing them to the finished films, and I'm very happy to have these two published and look forward to seeing this volume on my shelf. I hope you enjoy them. But all scripts are better, I believe, off the page and onto the screen, with eyes and faces on the words, and people all around you in the dark watching something real happening . . .

Don Roos
May 2000
Hollywood, California

Bounce

Bounce was first released in the United States by Miramax Films in November 2000.

MAIN CAST

BUDDY AMARAL	Ben Affleck
ABBY JANELLO	Gwyneth Paltrow
MIMI PRAEGER	Natasha Henstridge
JANICE GUERRERO	Jennifer Grey
GREG JANELLO	Tony Goldwyn
JIM WELLER	Joe Morton
BEN MANDEL	David Paymer
SCOTT JANELLO	Alex D. Linz
DONNA	Caroline Aaron

MAIN CREW

Directed by	Don Roos
Written by	Don Roos
Produced by	Bobby Cohen
	Harvey Weinstein
Original Music by	Mychael Danna
Cinematography by	Robert Elswit
Film Editing by	David Codron
Casting	Sharon Klein
	Patrick Rush
Production Design by	David Wasco
Art Direction	Daniel Bradford
Costume Design	Peter Mitchell

FADE IN:
EXT. CHICAGO SKYLINE (AERIAL) – DAY

Skyscrapers poking into clouds. A late afternoon in December.

EXT. CHICAGO STREET – DAY

A guy in his early thirties waits with a small group outside a Holiday Inn by the interstate for the shuttle to take him to the airport. He looks at the sky anxiously: snow? He checks his watch and, as he looks up, he sees a limo pass him.

THE GUY'S POV – THE LIMO

. . . eases onto I-90.

EXT. I-90 WEST TO O'HARE AIRPORT, CHICAGO, ILLINOIS – DAY

Snow is starting to stick to the roadway now. A MAN by a stuck car is flagging down a tow truck. We PICK OUT one car, a limousine, and then ONE VOICE, casual, somewhere between contented and smug:

BUDDY'S VOICE
What do you think happened?. . . You're kidding me. That's what you think happened? You really think that?

INT. LIMO – (MOVING) – DAY

BUDDY AMARAL, early thirties, is on a cell phone. He's drinking but not drunk, not what he would call drunk. As a result of a lifetime of things going his way, Buddy's a happy guy. His deals always close, his girlfriends always open; he will never be audited. Lucky. With him it's fifty-fifty at best: there's a decent guy inside, but it's hard to hate him. If you're a woman he's like your kid brother, the total pain who sometimes says, 'You look nice in that dress.' If you're a guy, he's your second pick for any team. Not your first, because you don't want him to think you need him. But second, because he'll fight like hell and pretend to not notice your fumbles.

                         BUDDY
                       (into phone)
You scare too easy, you know that, Jim? You're like . . . I don't know. Someone who scares too easy. He loves us. He fucking loves us.

As he talks, Buddy changes out of his dress shirt into a sweater; he kicks off his shoes, slips on loafers . . .

You want a quote? 'I can't see why we would ever leave.' He had tears in his voice; I thought he was gonna give me a corsage. I got the signed contract right here.

On the seat next to him is a stack of documents. We see the Infinity Air logo on the stationery; it's also on the luggage tags on Buddy's luggage.

I'm on their six o'clock flight – I'm comped for life, I'm telling you, they would've put me in the fucking cockpit but the seats are smaller and there's no movie. Anyway, I'll see you tomorrow morning, okay? Hey. My pleasure. You, too.

EXT. O'HARE AIRPORT – DAY

Almost dusk. The snow plows are now out in force.

INT. O'HARE – INFINITY TERMINAL – NIGHT

The departures board: two Infinity flights to Los Angeles are listed. The 4.00 p.m. reads CANCELED; *the 6.00 p.m. (Flight 82) reads* DELAYED. *There's a long line at the check-in desk and the waiting area's packed. We HEAR an announcement:*

                      ANNOUNCER (V.O.)
                     (over P.A. system)
Would those passengers confirmed on Flight 82 to Los Angeles willing to accept travel vouchers for a later flight please make themselves known to any Infinity employee? Thank you.

Buddy is standing by another businessman, RON WACHTER, a friendly late-forties guy. They both squint up at the departures board.

BUDDY
Shit.

WACHTER
O'Hare. Hell with runways and a coupla TCBYs. L.A.?

BUDDY
Shows, huh?

WACHTER
Think I flew out with you Tuesday morning. Ron Wachter.

BUDDY
(*didn't notice him*)
Buddy Amaral. Well, we'll get out. I've seen it worse.

Behind him:

JANICE
Hey, Buddy. You made it out.

Buddy turns, sees JANICE GUERRERO, an Infinity employee.

BUDDY
Janice. I was gonna call you.

JANICE
I was gonna hold my breath.

Wachter smiles: to be thirty again. He goes off.

Did we like your dog and pony show?

BUDDY
What can I say? Love at first sight.

JANICE
Lucky us. You on the six? We're just about to push it back.

BUDDY
Fuck. Got time for a drink?

JANICE
That's why they called me in on my day off. Drinks with the freight.

                              BUDDY
                  (*makes a telephone with his hand*)
Next time.

Janice knows what Buddy's like. Maybe it bothered her once. Not now: she smiles, lifts her hand up, too, flips him off. Buddy smiles, heads down the terminal.

EXT. O'HARE – RUNWAYS – NIGHT

Plows trying to keep up with the snow . . .

INT. O'HARE – INFINITY GATE AREA – BAR – NIGHT

Buddy's got two drinks in his hand, aiming for one of those tall bar tables where MIMI, a businesswoman, attractive, in her thirties, waits for him. The floodlights outside show the driving white snow. That, and the crowds, tell us that O'Hare is struggling to stay open.

Just as he gets to the table Buddy's bumped from behind by GREG JANELLO, the guy we saw back in town, waiting for his airport shuttle. He's in his early thirties, wearing a backpack and carrying a duffel bag.

                              GREG
Oh, sorry, sorry. It's this backpack. I don't know where I end.

                              BUDDY
Hey, you got the whole *Let's Go Europe* thing happening here. Youth hostels, Eurail pass, yogurt. Get high, see the Anne Frank house.

                              GREG
Sorry?

                              BUDDY
Join us. Want a drink? Sit down.

                              GREG
Thanks, but I just wanted to get something to eat. The line at the snack bar is –

MIMI

We've got nuts here. Oh, and I got these cheese things.

Mimi's already sized Greg up. Nice enough to share their table, but she'll stick with Buddy for the long haul.

GREG
(*looking at the crowd*)
Sure, why not? Thanks. Hi.

BUDDY

You got patches on those elbows? Let me guess. English teacher.

Greg takes in Buddy's cell phone, the Rolex, the casual, enormously expensive suit.

GREG

Let *me* guess. Agent.

BUDDY

Advertising.

MIMI

It's like agenting without the heart.

BUDDY

Am I that much of a cliché?

MIMI

Don't look at me. I'm just sitting here eating nuts.

GREG

And I'm not a teacher. I'm a writer.

BUDDY

That's how I started out. Couldn't make a living.

GREG

I write for TV.

BUDDY

Oh, TV? So that 'I'm so much better than you' look on your face when I said advertising, I must've imagined that.

7

MIMI
Maybe on his face you imagined it.

GREG
I didn't have any look on my face. Nothing against advertising. It pays me, I guess.

BUDDY
That's right. What do you do?

MIMI
I told you. I work for the National Organ Center. I'm in development.

BUDDY
She's in organ development. You gotta love that.
    (*he points to a small camera pouch on the table*)
You want to see David Crosby? She taped this speech he does about transplants and stuff.

GREG
I write plays, too. That's why I was in Chicago. Play opened.

BUDDY
What TV shows?

MIMI
Good for you. Where?

GREG
It was no big deal. Little theater.

Mimi picks up a newspaper.

MIMI
Really? What's it called? I'm here again next week. I like plays.

GREG
It closed. It was limited run. *Lilacs in the Dooryard*.

BUDDY
I don't even know why they have plays anymore. Hello, we have movies now.

Mimi has found the capsule review section. She flashes a sympathetic look at Greg.

MIMI

Oh. It's not in here.

GREG

Yeah.

BUDDY

What's a dooryard?

GREG

It's from a Whitman poem. 'When Lilacs Last in the Dooryard Bloom'd.'

BUDDY
(*to Mimi*)

What the hell's a dooryard?

MIMI
(*re: the bar; to Greg*)

Oh, they just put sandwiches out. Go on. We'll watch your pack.

He starts to leave, sees a big line at the bar.

GREG

Maybe I'll just check on my flight. Want me to check yours?

MIMI

Oh, great. Dallas.

BUDDY

L.A.

GREG

Hey, me too.
(*to Mimi, pointing to her newspaper so that only she can see it, for not reading the review out loud*)
Thanks.

He heads off. Mimi watches Buddy closing his eyes, dozing for a second. You can see her deciding to make him luckier ...

LATER

Mimi is fooling with her Handycam. She tilts up to FRAME Buddy in her viewfinder. He looks up from the review of Greg's play.

BUDDY

Jesus. When they don't like something . . .

MIMI

Oops. Here he comes.
(*as Greg arrives*)
We thought we'd lost you.

GREG

You're still scheduled for ten. They say it's gonna take off. Nothing for Dallas yet.

MIMI

It'll be tomorrow at the earliest. The airport hotels must be swamped.

GREG

Oh – take my voucher. It's for the Sheraton. The room's guaranteed. I'm going to stay here, see if something opens up.

BUDDY

You took a bump? When?

GREG

Just now. Hey, two coach tickets anywhere in the U.S. – or Mexico – and two hundred dollars. I went to Mexico for this show and I promised the kids I'd take them –

BUDDY

Two hundred? And coach?

GREG

Plus the hotel room. What? I should have haggled?

MIMI

He's pulling your leg. You did great.

GREG

Tell Abby. My wife. I just gave her the good news. I forgot I was supposed to work the Christmas tree lot tomorrow with Scott. Father–son Cub Scout thing, you know.

> BUDDY
> (*Is this guy for real?*)
> Oh yeah, one of those.

> MIMI
> Got any pictures?

> GREG
> Yeah, sure. Here.

He takes out his wallet, shows them to Mimi. Buddy starts playing with the video camera.

> MIMI
> She's very pretty.

> GREG
> She and Donna – a neighbor – they had these glamour shots taken at the mall. For a laugh, you know.

> BUDDY
> (*trying to be constructive*)
> Maybe it's designed for mall lighting.

> MIMI
> How old are your boys?

> GREG
> Scott's seven and Joey's four.

> BUDDY
> Hey look, smile.

> MIMI
> Jesus, are you recording –

> BUDDY
> Relax, I fast-forwarded. David Crosby's still here. Smile.

Greg waves at the camera.

> GREG
> Become a donor. Save a life. Listen to what Crosby said.

>   (*to Mimi*)
> What did Crosby say?

Mimi grabs the camera from Buddy.

>   MIMI
> 'Sorry I drank. Thanks for the liver.'

>   BUDDY
>   (*into camera*)
> We're here to celebrate the opening and closing of *When Lilacs Something Something Dooryard*, here with the author Greg –

>   GREG
> Janello. Greg Janello.

>   BUDDY
> And all I want to say is the critic for the *Chicago Weekly* is an idiot and an asshole –

>   GREG
> You read the review?

>   BUDDY
> And Abby, whoever you are, forgive him, he did it for you.

OVER THE LOUDSPEAKER, we hear a boarding announcement for Flight 82.

> Oops. That's me.

Mimi turns off the camera, puts it in her bag. She glances at Buddy ruefully. Greg notices.

>   GREG
> Men's room.
>   (*hand out to Buddy*)
> Nice meeting you.

He goes, saluting them both with two fingers to his forehead.

> Later.

He leaves. Mimi looks at Buddy.

                              MIMI
    Well . . .
                    (*hands him a business card*)
    If you ever get to Dallas . . .

Buddy looks at her, smiles.

INT. O'HARE – INFINITY GATE – WAITING AREA – NIGHT

Buddy comes up behind Greg, grabs his arm, and steers him toward the gate. He hands him his boarding pass.

                             BUDDY
    Here. Go sell a Christmas tree for me.

                             GREG
    What?

                             BUDDY
    Go ahead. I want the layover, if you know what I mean.
    Mimi? Organ development? Video camera? Think about it.

Greg doesn't talk about women this way, so he lets the remark slide. Instead he looks at the ticket.

                             GREG
    This is first class – and it's not my name.

                             BUDDY
    They don't check at the gate. And it's a comp.

AT THE GATE

Buddy and Greg have been waiting in this long line, talking. Finally, they're at the head.

                             BUDDY
    I told you, it was free. Enjoy.

                             GREG
    I really appreciate this –

Janice Guerrero joins the other Infinity employee at the gate. Buddy notices her. Damn. He smiles.

                          BUDDY
Hey.

                          JANICE
Hello, sir.

Greg hands her his ticket. She feeds it into the machine, hands him the stub.

                          GREG
Are you sure –

                          BUDDY
You're doing me a favor. Enjoy.

Greg heads down the gangplank. Janice has her hand out for Buddy's ticket.

                          JANICE
Your ticket?

                          BUDDY
You just took it.

                          JANICE
What?

She looks down, sees Buddy's name on the ticket she collected from Greg.

                    (*whispering*)
What the hell are you –

                          BUDDY
                (*to the other employee*)
Would you excuse her for a minute?

He leads her aside.

Now, Janice, come on.

LONG SHOT (MIMI'S POV)

Buddy and Janice are talking. Janice isn't happy about something, but she sighs, nods. Buddy turns, heads toward us.

MIMI

... getting into her coat, gathering her bags as Buddy walks up to her. He flashes something in front of her.

BUDDY
His hotel voucher. He insisted.
(*smiling*)
Don't you love air travel?

INT. AIRPLANE – (IN FLIGHT) – NIGHT

Greg has been drowsing; he casually opens his eyes. It's hushed, quiet, cozy in the first-class cabin. Cabin attendants are chatting; one of them, CAROL WILSON, looks over at him, raises her brows – 'Do you want anything?' – he shakes his head no. A couple of passengers – Ron Wachter among them – are watching movies on their private screens. He takes off his headphones, closes his eyes again. A moment.

There's a bump, a bounce. His eyes fly open. Then –

INT. O'HARE AIRPORT SHERATON – HOTEL ROOM – NIGHT

A dark room. The clock reads 2.15 a.m. Gradually we become aware of SOUNDS coming from outside and below. Many cars, trucks, and then people calling to one another. Commotion. Suddenly, bright lights go on outside.

The light wakes Buddy. Next to him in bed is Mimi. There are empty cocktail glasses on the nightstand. He staggers up, checks the time, looks out the window to see if it's still snowing.

BUDDY'S POV – OUTSIDE THE HOTEL

From the second story, Buddy can see lots and lots of camera trucks, taxis, people. A few reporters are already facing cameras, filing reports.

BACK TO SCENE

Mimi's waking up now.

MIMI
What time is it?

BUDDY

Something happened.

He turns on the TV, flips the channels until he finds the news.

TV SCREEN

'FLIGHT 82' is the video banner.

TV ANNOUNCER
(*TV filter*)
... here at the O'Hare Airport Sheraton, family and friends of the passengers presumed dead on Flight 82 have gathered to await bulletins from Infinity Airways. Once again, approximately one hour and eight minutes after takeoff, Flight 82 disappeared from radar screens over Kansas ...

Buddy watches, horror-stricken, with Mimi.

INT. JANELLO HOUSE, CHATSWORTH, CA – MASTER BEDROOM – NIGHT

The PHONE RINGS and ABBY JANELLO, mid-twenties, wakes up and fumbles with it. Abby's hair is trying hard to forget the mall perm it suffered last year; no luck yet. Abby's a good friend, a bad cook, a worse Catholic – a right-to-choose, on-the-pill Catholic, but one who'll still watch any movie with nuns in it. She's the type of feminist who's happy Gloria Steinem got contacts.

ABBY
(*into phone*)
Hello? Mom? What is it, is something wrong? ... Chicago. He's coming home tomorrow ... what? Oh, Jesus. They said Infinity? ... No, no, he took another flight. He called me ... Mom, stop it – put Les on. Is Les there? Yeah.

She's fumbling around the covers for the remote, shaken but keeping it together. She finds the notepad by the phone.

Les? Yeah. What's the number of the flight? ... Oh thank God, he's fine, he's coming in on Flight 31, L.A. – it hasn't even left yet. Tell her ... what's she saying? ... Well, maybe he doesn't know yet. He said they got him a hotel ... okay, yeah, I'll call you as soon as I hear. I don't want to tie up the phone, so . . . right.

She finds the remote, turns on the TV. It doesn't take her long to find the coverage. Her eyes are riveted to the screen. She dials another number without looking at the touchpad.

(*into phone*)
Hey, Donna? Yeah, I know. Look, can you come over?

THE TV SCREEN

. . . and the coverage of the disaster continues . . .

TV ANNOUNCER
. . . would be unlikely to have survived. Witnesses report seeing a huge fireball seconds after impact . . .

INT. HOTEL ROOM – NIGHT

Mimi's on the phone to her husband, her eyes on the TV screen.

MIMI
Yes, Roger, I'm fine, I just didn't want you to think I'd been rerouted through L.A. or anything. I'm at the airport . . . I don't have a number – I'll call you as soon as I know what flight I'm on . . . Well, they're not saying it was weather-related, are they? . . . Okay. Yeah, me too.

She hangs up as Buddy comes out of the bathroom.

You gotta call anyone?

BUDDY
(*holding up a cell phone*)
Done. Jesus. Look at me, I'm shaking. That could've been me.

MIMI
That poor guy's wife and kids.
(*off Buddy's look*)
Greg. The guy you switched with.

                              BUDDY

Shit, yeah.
                         (*as he realizes*)
They're not going to know he was on there.

INT. JANELLO HOUSE – KITCHEN – NIGHT

DONNA HEISEN, a believer in everything except pessimism, brings coffee to Abby, who's on the phone. They both whisper to avoid waking the children.

                              ABBY

Janello, Greg. Is he on that flight? You sure? Yes, that's right, Flight 31, that leaves when? Okay, thank you, thank you.

She hangs up. Donna smiles.

                              DONNA

See? So you can relax.

                              ABBY

I just wish he'd call.

                              DONNA

He's asleep. You don't get news reports when you're asleep.

                              JOEY
                        (*from the doorway*)

Mommy?

They both turn to see JOEY JANELLO, four years old, in the doorway.

                              ABBY

Hey, big guy, what are you doing up?

                              JOEY

Can I watch TV?

                              DONNA

It's the middle of the night, silly. Come on, let Aunt Donna tuck you back in, 'kay?

                              ABBY

I'll take him. Come on, Joey.

18

CAMERA FOLLOWS ABBY as she walks down the hallway and into:

INT. JANELLO HOUSE – BOYS' BEDROOM – NIGHT

SCOTT, seven years old, is asleep. She puts Joey in bed, tucks him in. She looks at them both. Somehow there's a part of her that knows she'll never get back to this moment, when her children are sleeping and their father is coming home to them.

INT. O'HARE AIRPORT – INFINITY TERMINAL – NIGHT

Chaos. Buddy fights his way through the crowds, then sees the woman he's been looking for – Janice Guerrero, the Infinity gate clerk . . .

BUDDY
Janice!

She sees him. Her eyes are red.

JANICE
Oh my God, Buddy . . . I knew three girls on that crew, and the copilot –

BUDDY
We got a problem. The roster's not right.

Janice looks shocked as she remembers.

JANICE
Oh, Jesus. Who was he?

BUDDY
You gotta get into the system. Can you do that?

INT. JANELLO HOUSE – BATHROOM – DAY

It's early morning. Abby is wild, red-eyed, washing her face. Donna is trying to cover her own nervousness.

ABBY
What time is it in Chicago?

DONNA
It's nine.

ABBY
Jesus, Donna, where the hell is he?

Scott comes to the bathroom door.

SCOTT
There's somebody at the door.

INT./EXT. JANELLO HOUSE – FOYER/FRONT DOOR – DAY

Abby opens the door. A man and a woman with sad, kind faces stand on the porch.

KEVIN (MAN)
Mrs. Janello?

ABBY
Are you from the airline?

KEVIN
Yes. I'm Kevin Walters and this is Ellen Seitz. Ma'am –

ABBY
He said he was taking a later flight.

ELLEN (WOMAN)
When was the last time you spoke to him?

ABBY
Last night, about eight.

KEVIN
Ten p.m. Chicago.

ELLEN
We have conflicting manifests. One of them – we can't tell yet if it's accurate or not – one of them lists your husband on Flight 82.

ABBY
Well, *I* know. He got bumped. That's what he said.

KEVIN
We have a crisis center at LAX. That's where the first news will be.

                         ABBY
   Just a minute.

She closes the door. From behind her:

                         DONNA
   We'll go together. Jack can watch the boys.

Abby turns to see Donna, whose eyes are full of tears.

                         ABBY
                    (*her voice tight*)
   Don't cry, Donna. You're the optimist.

                         DONNA
   I'm not crying.

But Abby knows better.

INT. AIRPLANE – (TAXIING) – DAY

Takeoff. Buddy is in first class. Everyone around him is nervous. He's drunk, gripping the armrest of his seat, praying as the plane taxis down the runway.

INT. AIRPLANE – (IN FLIGHT) – DAY

It's quiet. Buddy comes out of the rest room. Sees:

A FLIGHT ATTENDANT

. . . in the galley, sobbing quietly on the shoulder of an older ATTENDANT. The older Attendant meets Buddy's eyes. He looks away, guiltily . . .

EXT. LOS ANGELES AIRPORT – DAY

An Infinity 757 touches down.

INT. INFINITY TERMINAL, LAX – GATE – DAY

Buddy, pale, baggy-eyed, comes out of the jetway and into the terminal. JIM WELLER, Buddy's partner and quasi-boss, the older brother type, takes his bags, puts a hand on his shoulder. We see him ask, 'You okay?' Buddy nods blankly. They make their way through the crowd of reporters and family members.

Up ahead, they see a huge gaggle of reporters. There's a briefing room. He and Jim pass by.

Abby, also blank, sees them. They don't register with her. Kevin and Ellen usher her, with Donna, into another room.

INT. COUNSELING ROOM/GLASS OFFICE – DAY

A commandeered bullpen. Desks, bulletin boards, a desktop Christmas tree in the room beyond this one, a glassed-in office. A fax machine spits out an image that we can't see, but Ellen can, and she picks it up and looks through the window into a larger room, full of family members. She sees Abby and Donna sitting beyond. CAMERA FOLLOWS Ellen as she exits the office into the larger room. Abby doesn't see her until the last moment. She looks up at Ellen, who hands her the paper. Abby looks at it, then drops it to the floor, fumbles for Donna, who grabs her, holds her tight. WE DRIFT DOWN TO SEE A XEROX OF GREG'S LICENSE on the floor.

INT. BUDDY'S SANTA MONICA CONDO – DAY

Before dusk. Buddy and Jim come in. Buddy heads right for the wet bar, makes himself a drink, flips on the TV. It's carrying news reports about the Infinity crash.

Jim joins Buddy in front of the TV. He gently tries to take the bottle away from Buddy.

JIM
We got a big day tomorrow. Infinity already called. They want to get in front of this.

BUDDY
Yeah.

Jim puts the bottle on the wet bar, prepares to leave. At the door:

JIM
Glad you missed that flight, Buddy.

He leaves. Buddy, eyes on the TV, stands up, goes to the wet bar, sits down with the bottle again.

ON TV SCREEN:

The newsperson is interviewing THE MAN on page 3 who would've been on the flight but skidded off the road on the way, missed his flight waiting for a tow – and lived.

    MATCH CUT TO:

LIVING ROOM

Next morning. Buddy wakes up to the angry CAW a phone makes when it's been knocked off the hook. He shakes his head, finds the receiver, puts it on the phone. As soon as he does, the phone rings. He picks it up, listens to an urgent voice, nods. He swallows a mouthful of whiskey, gets going.

EXT. BUDDY'S CONDO – DAY

A delivered newspaper catches Buddy's eye. On the FRONT PAGE are several stories about Infinity and its fatal crash. Buddy flips through the paper – until he comes upon something that makes him angry . . .

INT. TANG-WELLER OFFICES (TANG 1) – DAY

Buddy is storming down a hallway in the offices of Tang-Weller, an advertising firm of thirty employees bursting its seams. He passes several employees; one of them points, mouths 'Conference room.'

INT. TANG-WELLER 'WAR ROOM' (TANG 1) – DAY

Cartons everywhere, menus from takeout places taped on the walls, a conference table that's really just a bunch of desks and tables pushed together. Obviously something is going on: Jim is in a huddle at the far end of the room, and storyboards and mock-ups cover the table. Buddy interrupts a small group by the door. He waves the open newspaper at KAREN, a team leader on the Infinity account, who's standing with LUKE.

BUDDY
Maybe I'm wrong, but I thought we were trying to create a consistent brand image in the public's eye. The typeface, the logo – who authorized this?

KAREN
Buddy, come on, it's just telling people who lost relatives what numbers to call, okay? It's not like tomorrow's ad.

LUKE
Hey, weren't you supposed to be on that flight?

BUDDY
Like I'd fly in that kind of weather.
          (*to Karen*)
What do you mean, tomorrow's ad?

Karen gestures to where Jim and another man, TODD EXNER, are talking.

KAREN
We're getting help. That's Todd Exner. Damage control, spin. Tylenol, ValuJet. Infinity sent him out here this morning to work with us on their condolence ads.

BUDDY
Condolence ads? Like, sorry we crashed the plane?

KAREN
He's been locked up with Josh all morning. But boy, they sure love my coffee.

Jim is rapping the table for attention.

JIM
People, please, we don't have a lot of time today. Todd?

EXNER
I'll be brief. I want to thank you all for your ideas. I'm going to recommend to the board that we go with the concept that Josh and Sharon have been working on –

KAREN
That's Karen, actually.

EXNER

It's based on a wire photo out of Chicago . . . I'm going to need someone to lock up the rights to this pronto –

He and JOSH, a go-getter, unfurl a two-by-three-inch mockup with a laser-printed photo in the center.

POSTER

Two Infinity employees, in tears, embracing. Behind them, a check-in desk heaped with flowers that people have left there as tributes. Under the photo is a caption: WE GRIEVE FOR OUR PASSENGERS, OUR CREW, AND THEIR FAMILIES.

BACK TO SCENE

It's pretty moving.

BUDDY

Are you serious? That sentimental, self-serving crap? We're not running that.

EXNER

Excuse me?

BUDDY

No one gives a shit how Infinity feels. Why should they? A plane crashed, fine, there'll be an investigation, it'll be some rudder or hydraulic line or static electricity stuff, whatever. Shit happens, to United, to TWA, to American. Why take responsibility for bad luck?

EXNER

I don't think we want to hide our heads in the sand.

BUDDY

Plus, you don't originate campaigns. Neither do you, Josh. We all do. Together. Okay?

JIM

Buddy, nobody's running the ball around you –

EXNER
(*directly to Josh*)
Okay, let's get on this. I want to fax a copy to the board by noon. *USA Today*, the *New York Times*, the *Chicago Tribune*, and the *L.A. Times*. Come on, let's go!
(*he turns to Buddy*)
People died here, my friend. Two hundred and sixteen people. You have any idea how much pain that represents? Maybe it's not Infinity's fault, but it happened on their watch. So we shoot this ad and run it tomorrow. And we edit the same kind of thing from news coverage and amateur video and run it on the network news tonight. So I guess my point is, get your fucking ego out of my way or I'll run it down. *Capisce?*

He leaves. Everyone gets very busy organizing the film shoot, the radio spots, the print ads. Nobody looks at Buddy.

BUDDY
How'd I know he was going to wind up saying *capisce?*

Karen flashes him a sympathetic look. Buddy leaves.

INT. VENICE RESTAURANT/BAR

A rainy December night. Half-assed Christmas decorations behind the bar. Buddy sees a young woman, FIONA, drinking. Buddy looks like shit but even when he looks like shit, he's better than the slim pickings at this bar. Fiona smiles back.

INT. BUDDY'S CONDO – NIGHT

You know the deal here: Buddy rolls off Fiona, unable to stay hard. She looks at him.

BUDDY
Sorry, it's not happening.

FIONA
Oh, it'll happen. It may not happen the way you like it to happen, but it's gonna happen.

Buddy looks at her, sighs, slides his body down the bed.

LATER

Buddy's apparently just told her what happened.

FIONA
Oh, God. It coulda been you. It shoulda been you, only you were a nice guy. So it's kind of a sweet story.

BUDDY
Two hundred and sixteen people died.

FIONA
Yeah, on the other hand, definitely. And in a plane, you don't just die. It's dying plus falling. I mean, isn't that like an inborn fear?

BUDDY
You want another drink?

He gets up, goes to the bathroom. The SOUND OF RUNNING WATER.

FIONA
But in a way I kinda think it could be nice. Because other ways, you die alone. In a plane you go with other people. You can hold the person's hand next to you. I mean, you can die in bed and hold someone's hand, but they're not on the same level. They're thinking, Shit, you're a goner and I'm not. Like, what am I gonna have for dinner? So dying in a plane's not pure downside. Hey, that's a joke. Downside. Hello?

No answer from the bathroom. She heads toward it.

INT. BUDDY'S BATHROOM AND STALL – NIGHT

Fiona heads toward the stall, opens the door. Buddy's slumped on the bench in the steam shower, drink in hand. He looks up at her.

BUDDY
What, you want cab fare? Help yourself.

Fiona leaves through the bedroom, furious.

WIPE TO:

SAME BED, SUMMER

This time it's Buddy and a second bar girl, SASHA. He's passed out. She sees his wallet. Takes the cash out of it and splits.

WIPE TO:

SAME BED, SEPTEMBER

Late afternoon. Another girl, obviously a pro, smokes and gets dressed. Buddy looks more than nine months older than the first time we saw him. Plus, he's had a few. He finds something in his wallet as he gets cash to pay her.

BUDDY
Hey. How much if we go out?

ZOLA (PRO)
Huh?

BUDDY
To a function. I have to be at a function.
(*he shows her the invitation he found*)
Beverly Hills Hilton.

ZOLA
I need something to wear.

BUDDY
What's wrong with that?

INT. BEVERLY HILTON BALLROOM – NIGHT

WE'RE SEEING an Infinity Air commercial on a huge projection TV screen. Sentimental music, the kind that makes Pachelbel's Canon sound edgy. This is one of the series of five 'We Remember' commercials Tang-Weller did for Infinity during the past nine months. It tells the story of one Infinity flight attendant (CAROL WILSON, page 15) who died in the crash, how her family coped, how they want what she stood for – Infinity Air – to keep burning bright. It sounds like too much, but it's done with enough skill to be effective.

The commercial ends, the lights go up, and we see we're in the ballroom of the Beverly Hilton Hotel.

LOUD APPLAUSE. That was apparently the last clip of the five nominated commercials of the year. Zola, Buddy's pro date, is SOB-BING LOUDLY. Buddy, really drunk now, is rolling his eyes. Jim, Karen, Josh, and Todd Exner are also at the table; no one seems delighted that Buddy could make it.

BUDDY

Makes you wish you crashed more often, doesn't it, Todd? Makes Infinity so damn human.

ZOLA
(sincerely, tearful)
They always find a burned doll. That's what gets me. And it's funny, you never see any dolls on planes that don't crash.

EMCEE
(at the podium)
And this year's winner for Best National Campaign is Tang-Weller, client Infinity Air, 'We Remember' series.

At the table, Jim gets up.

BUDDY
Hey, that's my account.

JIM
Buddy, please –

EXNER
Can't you control this idiot?

Jim tries to reason with Buddy, but Buddy stumbles on up to the podium, takes the award from the presenter. He stands there a moment, sweating, drunk, squinting at the crowd.

BUDDY
Thank you, thank you for this award. Gee, it's so heavy, aren't I supposed to say that? Or, 'Oh, so this is what these look like up close.' It's good to see you all. I haven't been around much this year. See, I was supposed to be on that flight. Isn't that ironic? I coulda been one of those people up there who believed so much in Infinity Air I was glad to die, just so's it could get all this great attention on how well it

handled it. Isn't that what we're saying? Hey, we crashed, but man, we're hurting and we're humble, and we're ready to sell tickets, right?

Jim is now at the podium. Into the microphone:

JIM
Thank you, ladies and gentlemen. Thank you.

He tries to lead Buddy off the stage.

BUDDY
Shame about the dead people, but hey, it's an ill wind, right? Blew us right onto the map!

He stumbles, Jim straightens him up, and then Buddy passes out, hits the floor with a sickening thud.

BACK AT THE TABLE

They're all stunned, humiliated. Except Zola.

ZOLA
Is there a party after?

FADE OUT.

FADE IN:

EXT. DESERT DRUG & ALCOHOL CENTER, RANCHO MIRAGE — DAY

TITLE: ninety DAYS LATER. Jim is walking Buddy to the car, carrying Buddy's suitcase. Buddy carries a canvas tote bag.

JIM
You should take your time easing back in. We're in good shape.

BUDDY
How can you be in good shape? I've been away for three months.

JIM
You've been away for a year, but who's counting. You look

good. Think it'll take? I mean, you feel good?

Buddy nods, looks up at the sky. A plane flies overhead. Buddy's expression changes slightly, but he forces a smile.

INT. TANG-WELLER (TANG 1) – NIGHT

The banners slung from the rafters tell us it's a welcome back party for Buddy Amaral. Buddy's in mid-speech.

BUDDY
I'm sorry I had to put you guys through this whole Twelve-step trip, it's so eighties, but you know . . . I feel better, I feel great. And I hear you guys've been busy while I was gone – Southern California Toyota dealers, that's great, Josh – and we got a lot of great things ahead – bigger offices, for one, so Jim tells me – and so, even though New Year's is a couple days away – here's to the future. Is this apple juice?
(*Jim tastes it, nods*)
I got my own taster now. Like Nero.
(*he holds up his drink*)
To the future.

BUDDY'S OFFICE

Later. Jim is showing Buddy a manila folder filled with photos of an office building.

JIM
Two floors, twenty-four thousand square feet, employee and client parking, and within one block two banks, a Kinko's, and a couple dozen Starbucks.

BUDDY
What's the rent?

JIM
Oh no, we buy. Already got a deal with the owner – he wants out of the landlord business. Old guy, not too savvy, he'll do it at one-eight – *and* without a broker.

BUDDY
When can I see it? Assuming you want my input?

JIM

Anytime you want – the tenants are already out. It's great, Buddy. You're gonna love it. Don't fight it because you were out of the loop. We didn't want to bother you.

BUDDY

Hey, Jim, come on. It'll be great. Really. Excuse me.

INT. TANG-WELLER MEN'S ROOM (TANG I) – NIGHT

Later. Buddy's washing his hands, looking at himself in the mirror. We can HEAR the sounds of the party through the door. His apple juice is on the ledge in front of him. Further down is another glass, abandoned, half-full of what looks like scotch. Buddy looks at it, sidles down to it, lifts it to his nose. From behind him:

SETH (O.S.)

You sure you wanna do that?

Buddy turns to see SETH, twenty-five, Starbucks-ish, not particularly ingratiating, standing at the urinal. He nods toward the glass.

BUDDY

Oh. Jesus – thought it was my glass. See, here's mine. Apple juice.

SETH

Right.

Buddy watches him in the mirror as he finishes washing his hands.

(*without turning around*)
You don't want to stare at me like that, not in the men's room. It's sexual harassment.

BUDDY

Are you kidding me? I'm not gay.

SETH

Yeah, but I am.
(*he zips up, comes to the sink*)
And you're my boss, at least officially, so . . .

BUDDY

Since when?

SETH

Since a week after they shipped you to Palm Springs. You had some breakdown during an awards ceremony? That's what I heard.

BUDDY

It wasn't a breakdown. It was an episode. So what do you do here?

SETH

P.A. Office floater. Handle the computers, mostly. You guys have some real Jurassic hardware here.
(*indicates the glass*)
Would that've been your first drink since they released you?

BUDDY

You got a lot of nerve, kid.

SETH

Relax, I'm a drunk, too. Six years sober. AA and NA.

BUDDY

And we hired you?

SETH

I had to sign a 'no-episode' clause, but yeah. Look, you want some help with your re-entry, I'm happy to oblige. Just don't screw up. Lot of nice people working here. Why should they pay for your shit?

BUDDY

Because I own twenty percent of the company? And in case you were picking pimples when they covered this at your rehab, alcoholism's a disease.

SETH

Yeah, you catch it from open bottles.

BUDDY

You're not going to make me feel guilty over something I had no control of.

                    SETH

Oh, so you're that type. When was the last time something was your fault?

                    BUDDY

I can't believe this guy.

                    SETH

They do AA where they dried you out? You know, the Twelve Steps, all that jazz?

                    BUDDY

They tried. I don't believe in God.

                    SETH

Man, he'll be crushed when he finds out. You're not going to last a week sober.

                    BUDDY

Fuck you.

                    SETH

Welcome back, boss.

He leaves.

                    BUDDY

P.S., you're fired.

But the door has closed and nobody's heard him. He slams the plastic glass onto the floor.

INT. BUDDY'S CONDO – BEDROOM – NIGHT

Buddy's in bed, lights out but awake.

INT. BUDDY'S CONDO – KITCHEN/LIVING ROOM – NIGHT

Buddy opens the refrigerator. Shelf upon shelf of diet drinks, apple juice, and Perrier. He goes to the living room. The tote he brought out of the treatment center is on the dining table. He dumps it out on the table. There's a copy of the AA textbook, Alcoholics Anonymous. *He flips through it.*

BUDDY'S POV – THE TWELVE STEPS

He looks at Step 8: 'Made a list of all persons we had harmed and became willing to make amends to them all.'

BACK TO BUDDY

Something about this grabs him. He thinks – then he searches – his bookcase, a basket full of magazines, his desk. Finally, he finds it in a closet:

PEOPLE MAGAZINE

The cover story: 'Flight 82. The Last Trip for 216 Very Ordinary, Very Special People.'

BACK TO SCENE

Buddy flips through it till he finds Greg's picture. We hear the SCREECH of a MODEM HANDSHAKE...

COMPUTER SCREEN

A Web site, a phone/address database. Typing appears on the screen: JANELLO, GREG. Buddy types in area codes: 213, 323, 818, 310. Finally, an address appears: 14398 Jewell Ave., Chatsworth.

Buddy stares at it.

EXT. JEWELL AVENUE, CHATSWORTH – DAY

Morning. Buddy is in his car, watching the door. He's about to get out when the door opens and Abby comes out, wrestling with a large Rottweiler. In the year since her husband's death, she's gotten a haircut. We hope she didn't pay much for it. The house looked better a year ago; the lawn is brown.

She wrestles the dog into her car and pulls out.

Buddy follows in his car.

EXT. STRIP MALL – SHERMAN WAY – DAY

Abby pulls into this strip mall, which is maybe two years old. Buddy parks across the street.

The mall has only one shop open for business, a dry cleaner with Spanish window signs. The rest of the building is vacant, two stories of mostly white-soaped windows.

Abby uses her key to enter one of the ground-floor storefronts. It has a sign on the door that reads VINEGROVE REALTY, *but above the door is a sign reading* COPIES. *Half these windows are soaped, half-mini-blinded.*

A moment later Abby lugs a sign out to the parkway, one of those signs that rotates in the wind. One side reads TODAY; *the other,* LEASING. *She goes back in the shop.*

ON BUDDY

In his car. The widow's alive; she survived; she has a job. She even has a dog. He could turn back now . . .

THE STOREFRONT DOOR

Later. Buddy tries to peek in. He breathes, decides, opens the door. It's locked.

> ABBY (O.S.)
> Just a minute!
> *(to the dog; urgent whisper)*
> Come on, boy! Back. Okay, okay, in here. There's your toy!

There are some STRANGE NOISES and then, finally, Abby opens the door. She's harried; a little wary. Her whole attitude says, 'Don't surprise me.' Her smile is tense.

> Hi. Hello. I'm sorry. I had to lock the dog in the bathroom. All of the storefronts have bathrooms, of course, which are large enough for storage. Hi. Abby Janello, Vinegrove Realty.

Buddy smiles, puts out his hand to meet hers.

> BUDDY
> Buddy Amaral. Hi. I was just driving by and saw your sign –

> ABBY
> Look, the dog's not supposed to be here, but my friend who was going to watch him – he can't be left alone – she has a

doctor's appointment. Everything's fine and then, you know. Involuntary urination.

BUDDY
Hope the doctor doesn't keep her waiting.

ABBY
No, the dog. Oh, you're kidding. Funny. This is a wonderful property. Are you interested? We got two units with a thousand square feet, and one upstairs with two but we can subdivide, that's not a problem. You want to check it out?

INT. STOREFRONT – DAY

Not much here: the old counter from the copy shop, a phone, a couple of chairs. The dog is throwing itself against the bathroom door. Abby doesn't acknowledge it, though the effort costs her. She gives him her spiel as she waves her hand in front of her, trying to dispel cigarette smoke. She picks up a Diet Coke can which is smoking; she rattles it to soak the butt inside.

ABBY
(*lying*)
I'm sorry, the last person I showed this to smoked. There's been a lot of interest in these units. Here's a setup and my card; I'm in between beeper numbers so ignore that. The building's two years old, very well built, with entirely new management. The comps in the area – we're about fifty cents a square foot less, and if you take one of the first two units, there's an additional discount – what business are you in?

Throughout this the BARKING has been DEAFENING.

BUDDY
Maybe if you let him out?

ABBY
Would you be interested in a ground-floor unit? There *is* an elevator if you'd rather be up.

BUDDY
What's his name?

ABBY
(*hesitating*)

Fred.

BUDDY

Fred?

ABBY

He doesn't like people and he's not trained, I've only had him a year –

BUDDY

It's okay, Fred. Good boy, good boy.

The dog stops BARKING.

See? I've got a way with dogs. And Rotties are great. I had one when I was a kid.

This is a mistake. How'd he know it was a Rottweiler? Abby is instantly on edge.

ABBY

Yes, they are. You know what, maybe we should do this another time. I'm expecting my boss any minute. Why don't you come back around noon?

BUDDY

Excuse me?

ABBY

I didn't say it was a Rottweiler. Okay?

BUDDY

I . . . I saw you go into the building, that's all.

ABBY

That was half an hour ago. You said you were passing by –

BUDDY

I did, I saw you on my way to a meeting, and on my way back I –

Abby has managed to get over to the bathroom door. The dog is BARKING AGAIN.

ABBY

I mean it! If you say one more word, I'm going to open this door!

BUDDY

You don't understand –

Abby opens the door and the dog bounds out, barking furiously at Buddy, its hair on edge.

All right, all right, fine. I'm sorry. I just –

ABBY

Get out!

The dog takes this as a command. He rushes for Buddy, jumps on him. Buddy tumbles to the ground.

Abby is SCREAMING, Buddy is YELLING, trying to keep the dog away from his throat with his hands. The dog rips his jacket sleeve off.

Buddy! Buddy! Stop it!

BUDDY

Hey, lady, I'm just lying here –

ABBY

Not you, the dog. Buddy! Buddy!

She pulls the dog off Buddy, manages to wrestle him back into the bathroom.

BUDDY

You said his name was Fred! I probably pissed him off, calling him Fred!

ABBY

(*still irritated*)

What was I supposed to do? You can't go around telling clients they've got a dog's name! Are you all right?

She is fumbling for cigarettes, lights one.

BUDDY

The jacket, the pants . . . Jesus. I didn't see a license, does it have a license?

ABBY

Look, I can't lose this job. If you make trouble, I . . . Please. You gotta let me take care of it.

EXT. BACK OF THE STRIP MALL – DAY

Two open doors – one to the store Abby was showing Buddy, one to the dry cleaners. Abby and Buddy sit on the curb. She's stuffing a freshly lit cigarette into the Coke can/ashtray. They are watching Buddy the dog sniff around the dumpster.

ABBY

I got him for the kids last year. They like him, it's just . . . He's a lot of work. And I think they kinda look at him as this booby prize for their father . . .
(*off Buddy's look*)
Oh. He d– He divorced me last year. We divorced each other.

BUDDY

Oh.

ABBY

I wasn't trying to buy them off, I swear. Maybe I thought it'd be a distraction. It worked better with Joey. He's five.

BUDDY

I was almost married once. Couple years ago.

ABBY

What happened?

BUDDY

Oh, you know. I don't know. Some couples are lucky and some aren't.

ABBY

Yeah, I know. We weren't too lucky. He was a TV writer – did you ever see *Midnighter*? It was syndicated. He did some episodes. I mean, he's still doing them, he's on staff now.

She has put a cigarette in her mouth. Buddy lights it.

BUDDY

You only took two puffs out of the last one.

ABBY

I don't really smoke. Last year I started chewing the gum, Donna was giving up smoking, and it sort of helps the nerves, and then I got hooked on the gum, and then I got TMJ, you know, from chewing, so this is just to help me quit the gum. I'm ten days off the gum.

BUDDY

Sounds like a good plan. By next week you'll be on heroin.

A WOMAN steps outside from the dry cleaners behind them, shouts 'Ready!' to Buddy.

ABBY

See. One hour or less. And here . . .

She takes out a deposit slip from her checkbook and rips off her address and hands it to him.

. . . When you get them rewoven, send the bill to me, okay?

BUDDY

It's fine – all right.

They both stand up. We see that Buddy's wearing a pair of bright sweatpants he borrowed from the dry cleaners.

Well. It was nice meeting you and Buddy.

ABBY

I was right. You didn't really want to see any space, did you?

BUDDY
(*holding up the manila envelope*)
Copies. The sign's still up. And then you launched into your spiel, and then the dog, and –

ABBY
(*mortified*)
Oh, yeah, right. Well. Sorry again.

He walks next door to the dry cleaners, goes inside. Abby watches him, then looks off at Buddy the dog.

> (*hand to her nose*)
> Oh, for God's sake . . . what the hell did you eat this morning?

She grabs a piece of newspaper, heads toward him . . .

INT. DRY CLEANERS – DAY

Buddy's behind a screen, changing into his mended suit. He hears Abby calling, 'Buddy! Buddy!' He sees her wrestling the dog back into the building.

INT. TANG-WELLER (TANG I) – BUDDY'S OFFICE – NIGHT

Empty office, except for Buddy. He's reviewing ANIMATIC VIDEOS on the TV, dictating his notes. He notices a folder on the coffee table; opens it: it contains the pictures of the building Jim found.

EXT. JANELLO HOUSE – NIGHT

> ABBY (O.S.)
> Joey! Five more minutes and I'm gonna come in and wash your hair!

INT. JANELLO HOUSE – KITCHEN – NIGHT

Abby is cooking dinner while Donna helps her fold laundry.

> DONNA
> Did you see a ring?

Abby flashes her a look as Scott comes in, opens the oven door.

> SCOTT
> You're not gonna get in. He locked the door. He said the bubbles are gone and you can see it.

> ABBY
> Honey, go in there and wash his hair, okay? Go on, go!

He leaves, goes down the hall. Abby waits a beat.

> No, I didn't see a ring. And I didn't not see a ring. I didn't look.

> DONNA
> Yeah, right. Was he cute?

ABBY

I don't know. Kind of. Not suburban. Not a soap-on-a-rope, Sears-Best kind of guy.

DONNA

I like soap-on-a-rope guys.

ABBY

I just hope his pants don't cost me an arm and a leg. They're lined.

Donna looks impressed. The phone rings. Abby snaps it up.

(*into phone*)
Hello? This is her, she. Oh. Yes, of course. Um, did you get an estimate on the pants?

Donna is all ears.

INTERCUT WITH:

INT. BUDDY'S OFFICE – NIGHT

He's on the phone, flipping through the real estate folder Jim gave him.

BUDDY
(*into phone*)
No, no, forget about the suit. It's business. You've got a realtor's license, right?

ABBY

Of course –

BUDDY

See, the thing is, my firm, Tang-Weller, we're relocating, and our current realtors aren't cutting it and I thought, you know, maybe you could help.

ABBY

Me? But I –

BUDDY

We've got seven thousand square feet in Culver City and we need like, three, four times as much. To buy, not lease. You think you can help? Somewhere under two?

ABBY

Million? Two million?

BUDDY

Yeah. What do you think?

Abby's doing the commission math on a pad of paper. Her share, three percent, would come to $60,000.

ABBY

But . . . why me? I don't have the experience.

BUDDY

You'll work harder. You're hungry.

ABBY

I'm hungry because I suck, okay? Look, let me have you call Norma, she handles all of this stuff.

BUDDY

I'd like you to. Can you come in Monday at ten? It'd be great if you had one or two properties to show us right then. Somewhere in the same area – Marina del Rey, Venice, Culver City . . .

ABBY

Wait a minute, hold on here –

BUDDY

There's only one thing. There's a property I want you to show us on Abbott Kinney. Have you got a pen? 18385 Abbott Kinney Boulevard. That's Venice. The guy's ready to sell, doesn't have a broker, so maybe you could book a double commission, you know? Can you set it up for us to see at eleven?

ABBY

I can talk to him, sure, but –

BUDDY

Great. I'll call you at your office tomorrow and fax over the specifics, what we're looking for, that kind of thing. You okay with this?

ABBY
Yeah, sure, fine. Thanks. Okay. I guess.

BUDDY
Great. Good night.

She hangs up.

ABBY
He wants to give me some business.

DONNA
I'll bet.

ABBY
I'm calling him back.

DONNA
Hey, he's interested, Abby. You're interested. It's okay. It's been a year. It's time.

ABBY
Yeah, time to make some money, Donna, that's all. God. Down, girl.

But she's intrigued – pleased. Donna watches her, smiles.

INT. TANG-WELLER (TANG I) – BUDDY'S OFFICE – DAY

Monday morning. Buddy, carrying a large glass-framed poster, bounces into his office only to discover Seth there.

BUDDY
Where's Judy?

SETH
Wichita. Her sister had an aneurysm last night. Dropped dead. Three kids.
    (handing him his messages)
She's there twice. Number two says she's quitting. Want me to get her for you?

BUDDY
Call her, tell her I'm sorry, send some flowers. I'll get her later.

                    (*reading a message*)
Yeah, tell Josh I got his third-quarter media plan and it bites.

                            SETH
And Jim's been buzzing about this ten o'clock you put on his calendar.

                            BUDDY
I'll handle it. And hide this. And the others in reception.
        (*pointing to Judy's 'Hang On – Friday's Coming' poster*)
And you can get rid of that now, too, while you're at it.

Buddy's off. Seth looks at the poster, which shows one of their campaigns for Infinity Air.

INT. TANG-WELLER (TANG 1) – JIM'S OFFICE – DAY

                            JIM
But I don't want a broker. This deal doesn't need a broker.

                            BUDDY
I know, I know. Look, it's just a couple hours.

                            JIM
I found the place! We're not going to find anything better!

                            BUDDY
You know that, I know that, so big deal. Look, she's starting over, you know. She's had a tough year.

                            JIM
Oh, she in one of your groups? 'Cause I haven't heard you mention them.

                            BUDDY
Anyway, we let her take us around to two, three properties, I've done my bit.
        (*as Jim hesitates*)
I know you want to be supportive.

                            JIM
                    (*not too annoyed*)
You can play that card once, pal, and you just used it up. Fine.

INT. TANG-WELLER LOBBY (TANG I) – DAY

Abby enters, looks around nervously. She's taken some time with her appearance. She goes to the receptionist.

ABBY

Hi. I'm Abby Janello. I'm here to see Buddy Amaral. I'm early. Should I sit down? Oh, sorry.

The receptionist, headsetted, is obviously trying to listen to a conversation in her ear. Abby looks at the framed ad campaign posters on the walls. There are three blank spaces where Infinity Air ads used to be. From behind her:

BUDDY

Abby? Hey.

ABBY

Oh. Hi. I hope you're not getting too optimistic.
(*off his look, she indicates the empty walls*)
You're packing already?

BUDDY

Oh, there was something wrong with the matte jobs. I don't think they were acid-free, which is key for matting.
(*a little awkwardness*)
You should always make sure your mattes are acid-free, otherwise they'll, uh . . .

ABBY

Have acid?

BUDDY

Exactly.

An awkward pause. Abby doesn't know they're waiting for Jim.

ABBY

I read the material you faxed me. About your business and your setup here. I don't know much about advertising. If you don't count *Bewitched*.

BUDDY

Well, we got our share of twitching noses but, with our drug-intervention program, that's on the decline. Joke.

ABBY
(*sincerely*)

Yes, very funny.

BUDDY

Did you find any properties?

ABBY

Yeah, I, uh, I have three, besides the one you mentioned.

BUDDY

The owner gave you the listing?

ABBY

Yeah, but I had to promise him I'd get him a higher price to make up for the commission. He's got a half-assed offer for one-eight but it smells fishy –

BUDDY

Yeah, look – when you bring it up to Jim, pretend you found it.

ABBY

Who's Jim?

BUDDY

My partner. Partner-boss, sort of. Larry Tate, remember him? He doesn't always like my ideas, so if you say it was yours . . .

ABBY

Oh, look, I don't know –

Suddenly Jim enters the lobby, a good-sport smile on his face.

JIM

Ah, you must be –

ABBY

Abby Janello, Vinegrove Realty. Hi. You must be Larry.

                              BUDDY
Jim.

                              ABBY
Jim. Pleased to meet you.

                              JIM
Hey, a friend of Buddy's . . . You two meet out in Palm Springs?

                              ABBY
No, no. I –

                              BUDDY
Well, we better get rolling. You parked on the street?

                              JIM
I've got the attorney meeting at 1.00, so let's take two cars . . .

                              BUDDY
                            (*to Abby*)
I'll drive us. That okay with you?

                              ABBY
Sure, okay. Great. I just left some papers in my car, so . . .

                              BUDDY
We'll meet you out front.

She gathers her things, smiles, leaves. Buddy thumps Jim on the sleeve.

Don't mention Palm Springs. It's anonymous, remember?

                              JIM
Did you make another Larry Tate crack before I came in?

INT. BUDDY'S CAR – CULVER CITY – (MOVING) – DAY

Buddy's driving; Abby's riding shotgun. She's nervous, rifling through her papers.

                              ABBY
Wow, he's picky. I thought he'd like that one.

                              BUDDY
Yeah, I think we're about to lose him. Let me see what else you've got.

>   (*flipping through her folder*)
> Tell you what. Let's go with this one on Abbott Kinney, and I'll look at the rest with you.
>   (*he pauses as Abby doesn't react*)
> What?

                    ABBY
Oh, it's nothing. It's just your compass. You don't see a lot of them anymore.

Buddy looks at the compass he has mounted on his dash.

                    BUDDY
Superstitious. Had one in my first car, never had an accident.

                    ABBY
Lucky you. Okay. So turn here.

INT. JIM'S CAR – (MOVING) – DAY

Jim's driving, following Buddy's car. He's on his cellular phone; he stops talking as he sees where Buddy's pulled in.

                    JIM
Shit.

They've stopped in front of Jim's find: the building in the Polaroids.

EXT. ABBOTT KINNEY BLVD., VENICE – DAY

Jim parks his car, bounds out to take Buddy's arm.

                    JIM
                    (*his eyes on the building*)
Buddy? Could I speak to you?

                    ABBY
It's okay, I have others . . .

                    JIM
                    (*undertone*)
This is the building.

                    BUDDY
Oh, you think so? Good.

                    JIM

No, this is the building. I mean, the one I want. The photos?

                    BUDDY

Oh. Wow. Well, I gave her the specs we were looking for – I guess there's only so much inventory on the market.

                    JIM

I'm gonna kill him, we had a deal and he went to a broker. We can't let her show it to us, we got to leave before his broker shows up – you see him?

                    BUDDY
                  (to Abby)
What time is the seller's broker due here?

                    ABBY

I'm the seller's broker. It's my listing. Exclusive. So I've got the keys right here.

She unlocks the door, breezes in . . .

                    BUDDY

What are you gonna do? Fate.

INT. EMPTY OFFICE BUILDING (EMPTY TANG 2) – DAY

Abby is leading Jim through the building. She's selling the hell out of it, trying not to worry about Jim's sour look. Buddy watches her. He catches her eye; she smiles uncertainly. He smiles back.

EXT. OFFICE BUILDING (TANG 2) – DAY

Jim comes out onto the street, followed by Buddy. Abby locks up, gathers her strength, approaches them.

                    ABBY

I'm sorry about this one – it was just a wild guess – I have two others for today and I can get some more together for later in the week –

                    JIM

Let's go back to the office and talk an offer. Goddammit.

He goes off to his car. Abby looks at Buddy, astonished and puzzled. He shrugs his shoulders.

INT. BUDDY'S OFFICE – DAY

Jim, Abby, and Buddy are in Buddy's office. Seth comes in and out with coffee, files, etc.

ABBY

Listen, I understand your disappointment, but you really didn't have a deal. The seller was bound to get some advice and believe me, no one'd let him do a deal this size without a broker or lawyer or someone.

JIM

So how'd he happen to find you?

ABBY

I approached *him*. Look, he's going to list at two-one. That's still under market.

JIM

He was gonna sell it to me for one-point-eight.

Abby takes out a kind of slide-rule mortgage calculator.

ABBY

Say you go in at one-nine. What are you putting down?

JIM

We were thinking thirty percent – of one-eight. And a fixed at eight and a half.

ABBY

You'd be tying up a lot of cash for a commercial property. I'd go in at twenty, twenty-five at the most, free up some of that money. Thirty percent at one-point-eight is what, 540K? I say we go in at twenty percent of one-nine, that's 380K, meaning we finance one-five-twenty at seven and three quarter percent – and I can source that cheaper for you – that's ten-eight-eighty a month. That's a difference of twelve hundred a month. You can pass that on easy.

Buddy watches her. She knows her stuff.

JIM
I don't know.

ABBY
You waiting for me to offer to kick in some commission?

JIM
Well . . . it's an easy deal. It's not like you had to knock yourself out for six months finding it.

ABBY
Okay. One point. That's a check for 20K at close of escrow. But that's it. Because he can get two-point-one if he wants to wait even two months. But hey, whatever you want.

She starts to stand up – but Jim stops her.

JIM
All right. One-nine. Bring it by my office and I'll sign.

ABBY
Oh. Well, thank you. Yes, I will.

Jim leaves. The door closes.

BUDDY
Wow. How long you been doing this?

ABBY
Oh my God, I don't know where the words came from. I feel terrible about lying, though.

BUDDY
You didn't lie, you just didn't tell the whole truth.

ABBY
Like I tell my kids, that's called lying. God, Norma's going to die. I mean, this is so out of my league. I always got the feeling she gave me the job out of pity.
(*she catches herself*)
My divorce and all.

BUDDY
Maybe this'll get you off strip-mall patrol.

ABBY

Wouldn't that be great.
(*casually*)
Why'd he think we met in Palm Springs? Is he getting me mixed up with some girlfriend?

BUDDY

I don't know. I might have mentioned you were a friend of a friend. Jim doesn't like realtors. I'm the salesman, I like salesmen. He doesn't.

ABBY

Greg had a thing against salesmen, too. He wouldn't let Scott sell chocolate bars for the school. Didn't want his kid selling anything. I mean, still doesn't. And now *I* am. Funny. Okay, can I write this up here? And thanks. I owe you.

Buddy waves her gratitude away...

INT. ABBY'S HOUSE – BEDROOM/KITCHEN – NIGHT

Abby's awake, 3.00 a.m. She pads down the hallway. Opens the door of the boys' room: Scott and Joey are both asleep. In the kitchen she puts some Swiss Miss and three packs of Equal in a mug, runs hot water onto it.

FLASHBACK – ABBY AND GREG

A quick hug and kiss from Greg one late night in the kitchen.

BACK TO ABBY

Blank. No tears. She just breathes.

INT. ABBY'S HOUSE – GARAGE – NIGHT

The light comes on and Abby comes out. She gets into Greg's car, a big, boxy Buick convertible with a bench front seat. Obviously she spends a lot of time here. There are magazines, a box of cookies in the glove compartment. It smells like him. She turns on the overhead light, switches on the radio and starts reading a magazine. We notice a compass, just like the one in Buddy's car, mounted on the dash ...

EXT. ABBY'S BACKYARD – DAY

It's a March day, and Abby and her neighbor Donna are cleaning out Abby's gutters.

ABBY

And on Friday, the deal closes and they give me a desk – with a computer and my own partition. You know. Instead of working at the floater's desk.

DONNA

Everything's about perception, you know? Suddenly you're perceived differently.

ABBY

Yeah, I'm perceived as the girl with her own partition.

DONNA

Oops, watch it. Dead bird.

ABBY

You've got gloves on.

DONNA

Your gutters, not mine.

Abby fishes it out, grimaces.

ABBY

It's kind of amazing you don't see more dead birds. Considering there's billions of them. Considering how often you see bird shit.

DONNA

Obviously they're going to go to the bathroom more than they die. Everyone does.

ABBY

Go to the bathroom? Honey, they don't go to the bathroom, okay? They shit.

DONNA

Do they pee or is it all one thing? Kelly asked me that the other day.

Donna is raking the crap that Abby throws down into piles.

ABBY

What I don't get is why this guy did it.

DONNA

Haven't we been through this?

ABBY

I know what we thought, but he hasn't called me since, you know, with made-up reasons. We had a forty-five-day escrow, I heard from him maybe twice – with legitimate questions. I've talked to his partner or boss or whatever more. Not that I care. It's too soon.

DONNA

It's never gotten personal?

ABBY

I know he's single. He knows I am.

DONNA

That's probably why he hasn't called. My mother said after she was a widow people were like scared of her or something.

ABBY

I told him I was divorced. Norma said don't mention death in a negotiation.

DONNA

Norma. Anyway, you're probably right. He's shy or scared and you're not interested, so forget about it. I mean, it's not like you can ask him for a date . . .

INT. TANG-WELLER (TANG 1) – KITCHEN – DAY

Buddy's looking at some storyboards with Luke; Seth's in the background fixing his lunch.

BUDDY

You're gonna have trouble with legal on eight. Forget it, let them tell us. Ship it.

Luke nods, leaves – and Buddy sees Abby coming his way.

Hey! What are you doing here?

ABBY

Well, um, I guess, in the area. Looks like the move is on track.

BUDDY

This weekend. Phone guys are over there now.

ABBY

And, uh – I wanted to, uh . . .

BUDDY

What?

ABBY

I wanted to thank you, so I . . .
    (*she pulls out a small tickets envelope*)
I got tickets for the Dodgers. I know you like them, I saw your coffee mug. They're for Friday. I thought we could . . . you know. Go. If you want. Or you could just have them. Both, if you're seeing . . . if you have a friend who likes them. I'm fine either way.

Buddy's trapped. He doesn't want to encourage her; doesn't want to hurt her either.

BUDDY

Oh. Well, thank you. But . . .
    (*sudden relief*)
Oh shit, Friday? That's too bad. We got a business dinner, these clients in from San Francisco. Otherwise. Sorry –

Seth heads out of the kitchen with his lunch.

SETH

No, that's been moved to Monday. Remember? And it's lunch.

He breezes on into the office. Buddy shoots him a dirty look, then turns back to Abby, smiling.

                          BUDDY
    That's great. Great. Dodgers, huh?

INT. DODGER STADIUM – DAY

Buddy looks down at the rows of seats, sees Abby. Does he really want to go through with this? Then he sees Abby preventing a man from sitting in the seat next to her, anxiously looking around for Buddy.

Buddy's not heartless. He goes down the steps to her row, calls out to her. Her face lights up.

INT./EXT. DODGER STADIUM – NIGHT

The Dodger game. Abby and Buddy watch, cheer. Buddy turns to look at her once, watches her total absorption in the game.

INT. DODGER STADIUM – CONCESSION AREA – NIGHT

Buddy comes out of the men's room, sees Abby in a long line for the women's room. So he keeps her company, chatting as the line moves slowly . . . The other women in the line envy her for his gallantry. She notices their envy; agrees.

INT. PANN'S COFFEE SHOP – NIGHT

Buddy and Abby are studying the menu. They've got a seat next to the rest rooms. A teenage girl comes out, trailing toilet paper from her shoe, heading back to her big date. Abby's out of her chair like a shot, menu in hand, runs behind the girl, steps on the toilet paper. The girl moves on unencumbered. Abby returns to her seat, struggling herself with the toilet paper on her *heel now, and opens her menu as if nothing happened. Buddy watches her. Some woman.*

EXT. PANN'S COFFEE SHOP – PARKING LOT – NIGHT

Buddy and Abby have closed down the coffee shop. As they leave, the lights go out. They walk to Abby's car. Buddy opens the door for her. They are both strangely reluctant to end the evening.

                          ABBY
    You want to sit for a while?

Buddy knows what's waiting for him at home. Nothing.

BUDDY

Yeah, sure.

She gets in, leans across the bench front seat, flips up the passenger door lock. Buddy gets in.

INT. ABBY'S CAR – (STATIONARY) – NIGHT

Buddy settles in, studies the car.

BUDDY

This isn't yours, is it?

ABBY

It's Greg's. My . . . ex. Mine's in the shop, so . . .

Buddy notices the compass. He gives it a twirl.

Sitting in cars at the diner. I never did that, did you?

BUDDY

No, not really. No diners. Bars.

ABBY

How much of our life do we spend looking at dashboards, when you think about it? Dashboards and TV. And acoustic ceilings.

BUDDY

Too much.

ABBY

I had a baby in a car. Joey. Well, not exactly in the car, we made it to the ER. Not this car, it was a Gremlin, remember those? I had it in school. And I was . . . Greg was driving and I just knew I was gonna have this baby, and he wouldn't pull over, and I got this idea in my head that I didn't want to have the baby in the front seat, that it wouldn't be safe, so I tried to climb into the back, and I broke Greg's nose with my foot. I had a contraction and pow, I got him right there. And he couldn't drive, I mean, the blood was pouring, so I had to the rest of the way, screaming and crying and driving. God.

And he had a beautiful nose. A good face, you know, handsome, but a beautiful nose. That's all I could think of the whole time I was delivering: I ruined his nose. And later – he didn't know he did this – whenever we'd have a fight, he'd touch his nose, like Danny Kaye in *White Christmas* with the arm. Like, 'You owe me, pal.' It used to make me so angry.

She's smiling – and then looks at Buddy, who's staring at her like she's some kind of miracle.

What?

BUDDY
I just . . . I don't know how women get so brave. That's all.

ABBY
You think that's brave? I was so scared. I'm always scared.

BUDDY
It's not brave if you're not scared.

Abby takes this in, touched. It's maybe the nicest thing anyone's ever said to her.

ABBY
Well. You have a good face, too.

She touches his face. Suddenly, it's impossible to tell who moves first, who is kissing whom. But they kiss, a long, lingering kiss that surprises them both. It's just as hard to tell who pulls back first.

Thank you. Well, okay. Good night.

Buddy looks stunned – and like he wants to take it all back.

BUDDY
Okay, well. Thanks for the tickets. Good night.

He gets out, walks to his car, worried.

INT. BUDDY'S CONDO – NIGHT

Buddy comes in. He's shaken. He goes to the refrigerator, looks for something to drink. Searches the kitchen for some booze, looks in the wet bar. Nothing. He gets his bearings, calms down, just tries to listen to his own breathing for a while.

INT. TANG-WELLER OFFICES (TANG 2) – BUDDY'S OFFICE – DAY

Monday. Most of the support staff has been working all weekend. Buddy comes in to see Seth setting up their offices.

BUDDY
What do you think?

SETH
It's fine. You get a window, I get to work for someone who gets a window. What are you doing in here anyway? It's not even eight.

BUDDY
So I'm early.

SETH
How'd the date go with the realtor?

BUDDY
Fine, I guess.

SETH
Fine, huh? I thought she seemed nice. What happened?

BUDDY
What is this, Gay Confidante Day? Want me to hang on while you get your blow-dryer?

SETH
Hey, I don't give a shit, I'm just making conversation.

BUDDY
Well, it went fine but I'm not interested. So if she calls, just take a message. Say I'm out or busy and I'll get back to her.

SETH
And if she calls back?

BUDDY
Just keep taking messages. She'll figure it out.

SETH

That's what I like about working for you. The total freedom from hero worship. It's refreshing.

INT. TANG-WELLER (TANG 2) – BUDDY'S OFFICE – DAY

BUDDY
(*on the phone*)
Hey, you're the client, we'll sell anything. I'm just saying these new products aren't in sync with your brand positioning –

SETH
It's Jim on three. Urgent.

BUDDY
(*into phone*)
Yeah, look, I gotta call you back.
(*punches line three*)
Jim?

INT. VENICE BAR/RESTAURANT – DAY

Abby's on her cell phone.

ABBY
No, it's Abby. Abby Janello. Hi.

INT. OFFICE – DAY

Buddy looks into his outer office. Seth won't look at him, just keeps working.

BUDDY
Hey. How are you? I had a good time Friday night.

ABBY
Good, that's great. Look, I'm just across the street, I got some more keys from the seller to that closet downstairs. Why don't you let me buy you a drink? Celebrate your moving in. Bring Jim.

BUDDY
He's in a meeting and I don't drink.

> (*a beat as he decides*)

Ten minutes.

He gets up and leaves, passing Seth in the outer office.

You don't know what you're messing with. It's not funny.

Seth watches him. He frowns. Maybe Buddy's right ...

INT. VENICE RESTAURANT/BAR – DAY

Buddy comes in, full of determination to tell her. He sees her at a table; she's working on some papers. He watches her a moment. Then she looks up, sees him. He approaches her table tensely; his mouth smiles but not his eyes.

ABBY
Hi. I ordered you a club soda. Is that okay?

BUDDY
Yeah. Great.

ABBY
My husband didn't drink either. Not once, not even champagne at our wedding.

BUDDY
Oh, I used to. I just don't anymore.

ABBY
Oh. AA?

BUDDY
Yeah. Six months.

ABBY
That's great. Meetings and everything?

BUDDY
When I have time.

ABBY
Oh. The keys. Here. That one's for the furnace room, he forgot that Thursday.

> *(she's at a loss; this isn't going well)*
> My uncle was in AA. But he was like a really bad drunk.

BUDDY

So was I.

ABBY

I'm sorry, I don't know why I said that.

BUDDY

But the drinking wasn't the worst. It was thinking I was such hot stuff, you know. I've always been one of those, you know. Born salesmen. A closer. A people person.

ABBY

Ew.

BUDDY

But I wasn't, not even close. It's like how everyone thinks they have a good sense of humor. Or good taste. Or they're good drivers. And there I'd be, driving along thinking, Hey, I'm a fucking great driver, and I'd happen to look in the rearview mirror and there'd be all these wrecked cars and bleeding people in the street and I'd be like, Wow, there's a lot of bad drivers in this neighborhood. That was me with people. And I'd like to think I've wised up a little, but I don't know.

Abby's face falls a little as she hears this.

ABBY

Yeah, I get it. You're bad with relationships.
> *(she stands up)*
> And as someone who's standing in the street ahead of you, thanks. I'll be getting on the sidewalk now.

She drinks her drink all at once, starts to leave.

BUDDY

Wait a minute, Abby.

ABBY

I . . . I took a shot, I'm sorry, I misread stuff. I'm just grateful about you throwing me the sale and all that and fine. Okay? Good-bye.

She leaves. Buddy tries really hard not to follow her.

EXT. RESTAURANT – SIDEWALK – DAY

Buddy runs up to Abby, who's walking, half running, to her car.

BUDDY
Abby! Wait! Please.

He grabs her arm. She stops, turns to him, angry.

ABBY
I'm not divorced, Buddy. My husband's dead, okay? He's been dead just a little over a year and I should have been honest with you because it's too soon for me and way too soon for my boys. Just leave me alone.

He follows her.

BUDDY
I'm sorry.

ABBY
Of course you are. Everyone's sorry and no one's to blame. Except most days I think exactly the opposite is true.
    (*she stops, fumbles in her purse*)
Do you have a fucking cigarette?

BUDDY
No. Abby, please –

ABBY
    (*finding one, she lights it*)
I'm sorry about lying, but you see what telling people does? They get like you, all nervous. And I liked thinking of Greg and me as divorced. Everyone's divorced. It feels like some kind of decision we made. It was up to us, instead of fate or bad luck or chance. Plane crash.

She starts walking again.

BUDDY
Come on, let's go back inside and start over –

ABBY

Don't be nice to me. Everyone's nice to widows. You're the first person who's been nice to me in a whole year who didn't know my husband died. But you don't have to be the nice guy here. In fact, it's better if you're not.

BUDDY
(*stopping her*)
Abby, please. I don't think I'm the nice guy, okay, that's what I was saying. But . . . I don't want you to go. I like being with you. I like you.

ABBY

What is it you want, Buddy? Just tell me.

And looking at her standing there trembling, Buddy suddenly realizes he can't bear to lose her. He tries to explain it to himself:

BUDDY

I don't know. Your company, I guess. The pleasure of your company. Your input on video rentals, maybe. I stand there for hours, you know, staring at them. Someone to say good night to. The last call of the day. I don't have a last call of the day, do you?

It sounds good to Abby.

ABBY

Don't feel sorry for me, Buddy. I'm happy. Widow happy, anyway. Widow-with-two-kids happy. You grade on a curve, I'm happy.

BUDDY

I don't feel sorry for you.

ABBY

Okay. Well.

She looks at him. He leans over and kisses her on the lips. She kisses back, gently.

Then nothing with knives, snakes, or women who have to go undercover as hookers. The videos.

She smiles, gets into her car, drives off. Buddy watches her, scared and hopeful at the same time.

INT. ABBY'S KITCHEN – DAY

Abby and Donna are in the kitchen with SUE, a woman in her early thirties, thin but very pregnant. From the other room, we can hear a football game on TV. Abby and Donna are making a salad while Sue flips through the Multiple Listing Service book and eats carrots without pausing. Abby and Donna are at the sink, looking out the window at the backyard.

DONNA
Don't worry, I don't think he's getting bored, do you?

THEIR POV – BUDDY

OUTSIDE, Buddy and a bespectacled, balding man (STEVE) are talking over a barbecue grill. Buddy catches her eye, widens his as if to say, 'This guy's nuts.'

BACK TO SCENE

ABBY
(smiling at him)
Honey, it's a cookout. Of course he's bored. Aren't you?

Sue has joined them at the window.

SUE
Well, Steve can talk to anyone. I swear that's how he and Greg got most of their jobs. He's wonderful in a room, that's what his agent says.

ABBY
I guess I haven't been in that room yet.

Abby smiles as she sees Buddy feeding Buddy the dog hamburger off Steve's tray.

Sue, do me a favor and see if you can round up the boys. Follow that little trail of wingless flies . . .

SUE
(*leaving*)
Boy, the way you talk about your kids. I hope that doesn't happen to me.

ABBY
I can't decide whether to get that baby some booties or a gun.

DONNA
Well? How far *has* it gone?

ABBY
Nowhere. He's a nice guy. Nothing special. Except, when you come to the table, he does that little halfway thing, you know, like he's going to stand up. I love that in guys. Greg did that.

Abby sees Donna watching her, gets busy.

EXT. PICNIC TABLE – DAY

Steve and Sue, Donna and her husband, JACK, Abby and Buddy, Scott and Joey. Scott has raced through his meal.

SCOTT
May I please be excused?

ABBY
CD-ROMS, but no AOL, okay? It costs money.

BUDDY
Hey, have you guys got *Where's Waldo*?

SCOTT
I'm eight, okay? Come on, Joey.

Joey hasn't finished. He looks at his mother.

ABBY
Take it. But no drinks on the desk.

The two boys disappear.

SUE

Let me help clear, Abby.

ABBY

No, no, let's take our time.

SUE

I don't know how you do it, working and then those two. Are you going to get help?

ABBY

Help with what?

SUE

Household help? When they settle?

ABBY

Well . . .

STEVE

Honey, we talked about this in the car, it's probably not, you know, smart to talk about the settlement while they're still negotiating.

SUE

Why, so you don't jinx it? It's going to happen, don't worry. Oh, that's what I meant to tell you, Abby. I heard on CNN what they're giving the guy who lost his wife and kids –

BUDDY

So, when's the baby due?

SUE

Hang on – and that's not even a loss of income thing because apparently when she was alive she didn't lift a finger. So you should do a lot better. It was between one and two, you know. They don't care, it's insurance money, the whole thing's a win–win for both sides.
(*mouthing*)
Million. One and two million.

ABBY

Okay, okay, fine, let me just answer your question. I'm not going to get household help, okay? It's not that big a house.

                           SUE
      That was not his fault! You wanted to stay at home! Anyway,
      it doesn't have to stay small. You could put a wing on or go
      up, that's what I'd do, just blow out that roof.
                 (*noticing the looks she's getting*)
      Well, I'm sorry. When you can afford anything you want I
      don't know what you're saving it for. I wish we could afford
      some of the nicer things in life for our baby.

                           ABBY
      All you have to do is die, honey, you or your husband, all of a
      sudden and for no reason anyone can figure. Then you're
      dead and your little baby's rich and I don't have to listen to
      you ask about my fucking settlement every time I'm stupid
      enough to invite you over. That's what I call win–win.

INT. LIVING ROOM – NIGHT

All the guests are gone. Abby's in the kitchen washing up. Buddy's waiting in the living room with Joey, watching TV. He hears the noise of a plane crash . . . He gets up, goes over to a door leading off the living room.

INT. JANELLO HOUSE – OFFICE – NIGHT

Buddy sees Scott playing on the computer. Flight Simulator.

                           BUDDY
      Whatcha doing, Scott?

                           SCOTT
      Losing.

The SOUND of a plane crashing. Buddy comes closer.

                           BUDDY
      Is it hard?

                           SCOTT
      You can play. I'm done.

He gets up and leaves. Buddy knows he's been dissed. He looks around the room. It's been pretty much untouched since Greg's death. There's a picture of Greg and Abby on the wall; also Abby's glamour shots. From behind him in the doorway:

ABBY

Sorry. He's still angry. With me, his dad, Joey. He teases him all the time. Says he's going to die if Joey doesn't do what he wants. Oh, and scared of flying. Can't watch any show where they fly. I'm going to take them on a little trip soon. You know. Fly someplace close so if they can't make it back we can rent a car and drive. Good idea?

BUDDY

That could work. Nice office.

ABBY

I'm the kitchen-table type. This was Greg's. He and Steve used to work here. Nice computer, isn't it? It came two weeks before the accident, probably out of date already. He bought it to celebrate his play. He got this play on in Chicago. That's where he was, seeing his play.

Buddy's already seen a framed poster on the wall.

BUDDY

Uh-huh. *Lilacs in the Dooryard.*

ABBY

That wasn't the title I voted for. Who knows what a dooryard is?

Buddy runs his fingers along the computer keyboard.

Steve bought Scott *Flight Simulator*, thinking it might help with the fear of flying. But he just likes to make it crash. He knows I hate it so it's hard to resist.
 (*as she tidies up the desk*)
He was supposed to be on another flight. Even the paperwork in the beginning was wrong. That got me more than anything. You start thinking. The boys'd be getting ready for the bus and Donna would say, 'Oh, I'm just going down there, I'll drop them off.' And I'd like, I'd think, okay, which one is supposed to crash? Do I put them with Donna or keep

them on the bus? Which one is doomed? Or is the whole thing supposed to happen tomorrow? Crazy, huh?

BUDDY
Can I ask you a personal question?

ABBY
I guess, yeah.

BUDDY
Do you have a good attorney for the case against the airline?

ABBY
I think so. It's a group thing, some of the other passengers' families. I've got his card here. Why?

She removes his business card from a bulletin board near the phone. Buddy looks at it.

BUDDY
Would you like me to check him out? Have our lawyers ask a few questions about him around town? For free.

ABBY
Oh, I get it. You're after my money.

BUDDY
It's not just the money. It's what the money can buy.

She smiles. He knows he maybe shouldn't, but he can't help it: he leans in, kisses her. She kisses him back. They kiss for a while – they sense Scott watching them in the doorway.

Okay. Thanks for the cookout.
                (*as he leaves*)
Night, Scott.

We can HEAR him in the living room, saying good night to Joey. Then the front door closes. Abby looks at Scott. Suddenly:

ABBY
Boo!

He gives her a look of contempt, goes past her to the refrigerator. She grabs his arm, he pulls away, she tackles him, they end up on the floor wrestling. Joey comes in, sees them. A beat, then he piles on top . . .

EXT. ABBY'S HOUSE – NIGHT

About to get in his car, Buddy hears the screams and laughter from inside the house. It gets to him a little. That's the family he screwed up. Maybe still screwing up.

INT. TANG-WELLER (TANG 2) – KITCHEN – DAY

Buddy looks like hell; he's had a sleepless night. As he pours himself a cup of coffee, Jim pops his head in.

JIM
Where've you been? I've been looking for you.

BUDDY
Here. I've been here. You see that creative brief Josh is pushing? Crap.

JIM
We had a meeting with Pat Dorian? The Canner Group?
(*off his blank look*)
You know. Publishing, broadcasting, advertising. They want to add us to their little family.

BUDDY
Are we up for adoption?

JIM
You tell me.

He opens a folder, gives Buddy a look at the top sheet. Buddy's impressed.

BUDDY
You're shitting me. This is real? When did this happen?

JIM
They were sniffing around when you were out in Palm Springs. They're interested. Fact, I had to run the real estate deal by them unofficially, see if it made sense to them.

BUDDY

When were you going tell me? I'm a fifth of the company here.

JIM

Look, nothing's going to happen without your approval. But personally, I approve of being made a millionaire. So should you. We'll bring this to the board Tuesday. What are you doing for lunch? Bring a calculator.

BUDDY

No, I got a thing – I gotta do a favor for a friend.

JIM

Tomorrow then. Great day, huh?

He smiles. Buddy tries to smile back.

INT. RECEPTION AREA – LAWYER OFFICES – DAY

Buddy and Abby waiting.

ABBY

I'm not sure I want to separate us from the rest of the families.

BUDDY

You tell him what's been going on and let him give you his advice.

ABBY

I just think the guy we have now is kind of sleazy. I get the feeling he just wants to stick it to the airline. I have to keep telling him Greg's name.

BUDDY

Ben!

Buddy stands as he sees BEN MANDEL come into the reception area. Ben's fatherly but tough. Abby stands, too, nervous.

MANDEL

Buddy. Good to see you. This must be Mrs. Janello.

Abby smiles.

ABBY
Hi. It's nice of you to see us. I just –

MANDEL
I'm seeing *you*, Mrs. Janello, and you alone. I can't and won't ever disclose any of our conversations or decisions to any third party. As far as I'm concerned, Buddy's participation in this case is limited to the introduction we've just had.
(*to Buddy*)
If you'd like to wait –

BUDDY
Right. Call me at home when you're done. Good luck.

INT. CONFERENCE ROOM

Mandel ushers Abby into the conference room. He closes the door. Pours her coffee, which is waiting for them. Finally:

MANDEL
So. Tell me about Greg Janello.

INT. BUDDY'S CONDO – NIGHT

Buddy opens the door. Abby is standing there, emotional, raw, barely in control.

ABBY
Fuck him. Just fuck him. Can I come in?

BUDDY
Ben? What did he say? Come in.

Abby enters, pacing furiously, tears on her cheeks.

ABBY
God, I'm so angry, so angry . . .

BUDDY
(*alarmed*)
Abby, please. Calm –

ABBY
Don't tell me to calm down. Everyone tells me to calm

down! This is calm! This is as calm as you get when your husband blows up in midair.

Buddy's looking through the cabinets for something to offer her. Nothing.

BUDDY

I got water or Coke.

ABBY
(*shaking her head*)
Do you know what my mother said when Greg died? 'When God closes a door he opens a window.' You believe that? Like that's a comfort. What's he doing fucking with my doors and windows anyway? He's got a whole universe, let him open his own doors and windows.

BUDDY

I had a girlfriend who used to say when God closes a door he turns on the gas. Here.

He hands her a glass of water.

ABBY

I don't even know why I'm doing this lawsuit. For the boys, I guess. We had some life insurance but . . . why shouldn't someone pay? Someone should pay. They don't even know what caused it . . .
(*getting control of herself*)
I'm sorry, have you got time for this? I couldn't go home.

BUDDY

Yeah, sure, sit down. Please.

ABBY

He wanted to know about Greg. Greg and the boys. Everything that happened, how I found out, how I told the boys, everything. I think he wanted me to cry or get angry so I'd make a good witness, so he could tell if I had the stomach for a fight.

BUDDY

So you're angry, that's not the worst thing –

ABBY

You think this is angry? This isn't angry, this is nothing. I don't let myself get angry. If I do, if I really let myself go there, I don't think I'll ever get back. And I have to get back, you know, for my boys. So I keep it here. Irritable. That's what losing someone does to you. You get cranky. Everything irritates the shit out of you. Like my mother. Even Donna, who's been so good. 'Only the plane crashed, sweetie. You gotta bounce.' That was Donna's take on it. And that's what I've been doing. Bouncing. It's like crashing except you get to do it again and again. Oh my God.

She's seen the TV, which is MUTED. It's playing some syndicated drama show.

This is *Midnighter*. This was Greg's show.

BUDDY

Really, I was just flipping around –

ABBY

The one with the Vietnam vet – we got our new couch with this episode. God, what a stupid show. And he knew it, but to see him kind of talk himself into it . . . it used to depress me a little.

BUDDY

You gotta do that, you gotta psych yourself up for it.

ABBY

Don't do that – don't take his side. Now that he's dead everyone takes his side and I don't even recognize who they're talking about anymore.

BUDDY

Sorry.

ABBY

It's not that he wasn't a good man. He was, a really good man, but he wasn't perfect. He was a little tight with money, for one thing, and he didn't want me to work. But the worst was – he wasn't this big confider, you know? He had secrets. Not other women or anything like that. But he kept things to himself. He liked knowing more than me. Little stupid things, like if he said yes to some invitation, he wouldn't tell me until the day before. Used to drive me crazy. He liked to surprise me, too. People who like to surprise you, I think it's a power thing, you know? Like, he'd give me surprise parties and I used to hate them, not the moment of the surprise or anything, but after the party, when you think, God, everything he said for the past two weeks was a lie. When he got on the flight – he called and said he was coming home the next day – he wanted to surprise me. So in the end I was right to hate his surprises.

(*tearing up*)

If I ever get angry, it's gonna be at him.

BUDDY

Abby . . .

ABBY

(*in terrible distress*)

I don't want to think of him as a good man. I want to blame him. Every time I hear someone say something good about him, it just makes me sick. It's so wrong to say this.

BUDDY

It's okay.

ABBY

Because I did love him. I really did.

BUDDY

I know, I know . . . Shhh.

Buddy puts his arms around her . . . then he kisses her; she kisses back. It's comforting at first, then more passionate, and then something they can't stop, and don't want to. And while they kiss and find each other, Greg's episode plays on, mute, behind them.

INT. BUDDY'S BEDROOM – NIGHT

Buddy and Abby make love.

LATER

Buddy's awake as Abby dresses behind him. She sits down to slip on her shoes.

ABBY
I have to go. Donna has the kids.

BUDDY
Abby, I –

ABBY
I know what you're thinking. I just want you to know, this wasn't about Greg. I wish it were, because then I might not feel so guilty. But it wasn't. It was about you and me, not him. But I'd understand if . . . if it seems like I'm trying to work something out about him. So, you're off the hook, okay? You don't have to say another word.

This is Buddy's out. But as he watches Abby dress, vulnerable and touching, he can't – won't – take it.

BUDDY
We still on for Thursday?

Abby is casual, hiding her relief.

ABBY
Yeah, sure.

He grabs her arm, pulls her to him for a kiss. She leaves. Hold on Buddy. He looks at the clock: 9.00 p.m. He gets out of bed, pulls on his pants, looks for his keys.

INT. BUDDY'S OUTER OFFICE – NIGHT

Buddy, weary, worried, is walking down the corridor toward his office. As he turns the corner, he's surprised to see Seth in his outer office.

BUDDY
What the hell are you doing here?

SETH
I was over in production – their network crashed. Don't tell me you're working late.

BUDDY
Lock the door when you leave.

He goes into his office. Seth watches him, aware that something's wrong. After a moment, he follows Buddy.

INT. BUDDY'S OFFICE – NIGHT

> SETH
>
> I've been meaning to say, you know . . . anytime you want to pick up a meeting.
> > (*off Buddy's blank stare*)
>
> You know. AA.
>
> BUDDY
>
> Oh yeah, sure.
>
> SETH
>
> You are going to meetings, aren't you?
>
> BUDDY
>
> God, I hate that you get to ask that question. I feel like a child molester. 'Are you going to your aversion treatments? Still getting the little shocks when they show you the Garanimal underpants?' Yes, I'm going to meetings.
>
> SETH
>
> Okay, whatever. What's that?
> > (*he looks at the storyboard*)
>
> Oh yeah. You approved this already.
>
> BUDDY
>
> I know.
> > (*casually*)
>
> You know, I was supposed to be on that flight, the one that went down.
>
> SETH
>
> Duh.
> > (*off Buddy's look*)
>
> We all know. The girl who comes around with the sandwiches at lunch knows. It's what they told us when you crashed and burned. It was the end of a speech that began, 'You all might be wondering why we haven't fired his ass yet.'

BUDDY
I gave my seat to someone else. I switched. Did you know that?

Seth instantly guesses how that's made Buddy feel.

SETH
Oh. Sorry.

BUDDY
That's not the worst part.
(*with difficulty*)
Abby's his wife. Widow.

For once Seth has no comeback.

She doesn't know. She just thinks I'm this nice guy. I've tried to warn her off. She doesn't believe me.

SETH
Maybe she'll believe *me*. You're an asshole. I could put on a slide show. How did this happen?

BUDDY
I felt guilty, like it was my fault – it *was* my fault – so I tracked her down to see if she was okay. I didn't even want to talk to her, but once I did, I just wanted to do her this favor and disappear. You know. To make amends. Step 5, right?

SETH
Step 9, and no.

BUDDY
Besides, she . . . you don't know her. She's a great person. I mean, courageous, funny, you know. A survivor.

SETH
We're all survivors. You're breathing, you're a survivor. When did that get to be such a great thing to be? What's next? 'She's an eater.' 'She's a urinator.'

BUDDY
She's not someone you get tired of. She's the first person I ever met, I'm more worried *she'll* get tired of *me*. I think back

to before I met her and I'm like, fuck. How could that pass for a life, how could I get up every morning for that?

SETH

Buddy –

Buddy's suddenly angry.

BUDDY

It's not my fault the plane went down! It's not like I wanted him to die! It was just this tiny little thing that happened, me giving him my seat. Why should I let that keep me from this person? I've been punished, all right? I've paid. I'm not going to give this up, too.

SETH

If you don't tell her, every word that comes out of your mouth is a lie.

BUDDY

I haven't lied to her.

SETH

Tell her. If she's this great person, maybe it could work out.

BUDDY

'Oh yeah, I meant to tell you, I'm the reason your husband's dead. Chinese sound good?'

SETH

Get in your car and drive over there tonight.

BUDDY
(*at his watch*)
No, the kids might be up or –

SETH

There's kids?

Buddy nods. Seth looks at him like he's the loneliest guy on earth.

I'm sorry, man.

BUDDY

Just leave me alone, okay?

EXT. MINIATURE GOLF – DAY

Buddy, Abby, Scott, and Joey. Scott and Joey are playing up ahead.

BUDDY
(*calling out*)
Good shot, Scott.

Scott shrugs.

He doesn't like me.

ABBY
He doesn't like anybody. It's the age. I'm sorry about the sitter. And I couldn't ask Donna again.

BUDDY
No, it's fine.
(*to Joey*)
Here, Joey, let me help. Okay, now.

He stands at the cup, his feet angled so they'll direct the ball in. Joey putts; the ball goes into the hole. Joey drops the club, runs around to check. He yelps with delight.

JOEY
It went in!

BUDDY
Good.

SCOTT
He did it, not you. It doesn't count if you have help.

JOEY
Hey, Mom, can he come with us on the plane?

SCOTT
Shut up, Joey.

BUDDY
What plane?

ABBY
Our practice run, remember? Palm Springs.

> (to Joey)
> I'm sure Mr. Amaral is busy this weekend.

JOEY
Our daddy died in a plane.

BUDDY
I know.

SCOTT
I think it's dumb anyway.

ABBY
We're gonna do it, Scott, okay? We'll be back home before dinner.

The boys go on to the next tee.

> We had to drive to the funeral, Scott just wouldn't get on the plane. I don't want them to spend the rest of their lives afraid to fly. Greg'd hate his kids to live like that.

That does it for Buddy.

BUDDY
I'll go. I mean, it'll be fun.

ABBY
I promised them the water park out there, too.

BUDDY
What, they're scared of water, too? Fine.
(*casually*)
It's a big plane, right? I mean, that'll be easier for them.

ABBY
I think so . . .

INT. AIRPORT – DAY

Sunday morning. Abby and the boys wait while Buddy talks to a female GATE ATTENDANT.

JOEY
What if the pilot drops dead?

                    SCOTT
There's a copilot, jerk.

                    ABBY
Don't say jerk.

                    JOEY
What if the copilot drops dead?

                    SCOTT
Then the stewardesses can drive the plane. They're all trained.

                    ABBY
Flight attendants.

BUDDY AND THE GATE ATTENDANT

The Gate Attendant glances sympathetically at the Janellos.

                    GATE ATTENDANT
And this is their first trip since?

                    BUDDY
Yeah. And they're nervous. That's the mother and I'm a family friend.

                    GATE ATTENDANT
Is she scared, too?

                    BUDDY
No, she's fine.

                    GATE ATTENDANT
I had a friend on that flight. She used to work for us. Let me talk to them.

MOMENTS LATER

. . . after Buddy has rejoined the family, they hear:

                    AIRLINES ANNOUNCER
                    (*over the P.A. system*)
Would the Gregory Janello family please report to gate 21 at this time?

Abby and the boys gather their things. She looks at Buddy.

> ABBY
>
> It feels funny, getting special treatment this way.

> BUDDY
>
> Yeah, but if it helps them . . .

He's looking green around the gills.

> ABBY
>
> Are you okay?

> BUDDY
>
> Yeah, sure. Let's go.

INT. AIRPLANE – COCKPIT – DAY

The two boys are getting a tour from the CAPTAIN, who is showing them the instruments.

> SCOTT
>
> So who sits in that seat?

He points to the seat behind the copilot.

> CAPTAIN
>
> Sometimes there are two copilots.
> (*reading his mind*)
> Not passengers, though. Sorry.

> SCOTT
>
> It's okay.

> CAPTAIN
>
> But if you want to listen to me talking to the tower during takeoff, you put your headphones on number eleven, okay?

> JOEY
>
> Do you have a thing for your drinks?

> CAPTAIN
>
> Yup. Right here.

JOEY

I can have all the Coke I want for free, right? That's how planes work.

CAPTAIN

All you want.
(*to Abby*)
Well, that's about it. It's an honor having you on board, Ms. Janello. We'll give you a nice flight.

BUDDY

(*whispering, ostensibly for the kids' sake*)
Is there going to be much turbulence?

The Captain takes him in with a practiced eye. Abby notices it, too.

CAPTAIN

A boat on the water. Think of it that way. I mean, that's what you can tell the boys.

BUDDY

(*a memory*)
Boat on the water, right. Okay, guys, let's settle in back there.

He and the kids leave. The Captain puts a hand on Abby's arm.

CAPTAIN

If you think it might help your friend, I can have him served a couple belts before we take off.

ABBY

He says he's not afraid of flying.

CAPTAIN

Uh-huh. Good luck.

INT. PLANE – (STATIONARY) – DAY

Abby and Buddy have facing aisle seats; the boys are between Abby and the window. They seem well occupied with watching the luggage being loaded on.

ABBY

You said you used to fly a lot. Why don't you anymore?

                        BUDDY
        Oh, I don't know. No reason. Shhh!

He wants to watch the flight attendant demonstrate the safety belt, showing the safety card. His eyes are fastened on her as if she's explaining the meaning of life. Abby smiles, then her smile fades. Remembering Greg.

INT. PLANE – (TAKING OFF) – DAY

The plane hurtles down the runway. The boys are craning to look out the window. Buddy is tense, tight. Abby reaches out for his hand, clasps it in hers. Buddy forces a smile.

                        BUDDY
        It'll be fine. Happens a hundred times a day at this airport.

                        ABBY
        Oh. I didn't know that.

                        BUDDY
        Boys okay?

                        ABBY
        They're fine.

                        BUDDY
        Whoa. There we go.

There's a bump underneath them. Buddy tries to hide his alarm. Abby sees it. Casually:

                        ABBY
        Is that the landing gear retracting?

Oh. That's what that was.

                        BUDDY
        Yup. Hundred times a day.

Abby smiles.

EXT. PALM SPRINGS AIRPORT – DAY

The kids get out of the plane, cross the tarmac. Buddy is white but relieved . . . they head to the rental car desk.

EXT. OASIS WATER PARK – DAY

Buddy, Abby, Scott, and Joey, looking like any American family. Maybe happier than most.

On one ride with a height requirement, Buddy and Scott go together; Joey sulks at the gate with Abby.

Abby watches Buddy and Scott as they go by. She smiles and waves, then puts on her sunglasses to hide her eyes from Joey.

Abby puts sunscreen on three male faces; it only gets in Buddy's eyes. He makes a big deal about it for the boys' sake. Even Scott laughs.

EXT. RANCHO MIRAGE – DAY

Late afternoon. Despite the sunscreen, everyone's bright pink. The boys and Abby are asleep. Buddy passes a sign for the Desert Drug and Alcohol Center. It's a cloud on a perfect day.

INT. AIRPLANE – DAY (IN FLIGHT)

A little bumpy. Abby and the boys are fine. Buddy's white, his eyes closed. Abby notices, smiles. To distract him:

ABBY
Hey, you awake?

BUDDY
Oh yeah, sure. Dozing. You can really sleep on a plane.

ABBY
Boys, you ready?

JOEY
Yep. Where is it, Scott?

Scott reaches into the seat pocket in front of him, takes out a baseball hat.

I want to do it. Okay, close your eyes and pick one.

There are slips of paper in the baseball cap. Joey shakes it up.

BUDDY
What is this?

SCOTT

You'll find out. Come on.

Buddy looks at Abby, who's smiling. He closes his eyes, reaches in, pulls out a slip of paper.

JOEY

Okay. You can open them.

SCOTT

Read it. We couldn't decide so it's up to you.

Buddy unfolds the piece of paper and reads what's on it.

BUDDY

Darth?

SCOTT

Yes! That was mine!

JOEY

It was my second choice, okay?

Buddy looks at Abby.

ABBY

The boys don't think the dog should have the same name as you.

BUDDY
(*touched*)
Oh. Well, thanks. That's great. And Darth's good, because he's black.

SCOTT

No, that's *your* new name.

Scott's delighted with his joke. Buddy laughs, a little uneasily. He's got to do something. He leans back in his seat so only Abby can hear him.

BUDDY

What are you doing tomorrow night?

ABBY

You tell me.

BUDDY

I have something to tell you. I don't think it's a big deal, but it's a little hard to say, so I got to tell you now that I mean to tell you, so you have to hold me to it.

ABBY
(*only half-kidding*)
If this is about how you've got a wife and kids in Playa del Rey . . .

BUDDY

No, no, it's nothing like that. You'll probably . . . it probably means nothing, I just want to tell you.

ABBY

Tell me now.

BUDDY

Tomorrow. Just . . . don't let me not tell you.

ABBY

Gee, this'll be a fun twenty-four hours.

BUDDY

It's nothing. Relax.

ABBY

Well, whatever it is . . . thanks for today.

BUDDY

Hey. Least I could do.

He turns to look out the window. Abby studies him, shrugs.

EXT. ABBY'S HOUSE – DAY

Abby pulls up to her house, as a woman at the front step is leaving a manila envelope on the mat. Abby stops the car, gets out.

ABBY

Can I help you?

The woman turns. We see it's Mimi, the woman Buddy picked up in the airport bar the night of the accident.

                    MIMI
              (*a little nervous*)
Are you Mrs. Janello?

                    ABBY
Yes.

                    MIMI
Now that I'm here, I wish I'd just mailed this. I'm Mimi
Praeger. Here.

*She hands Abby the note she just wrote. Abby reads it, then looks at the
manila envelope Mimi has in her hand.*

                    ABBY
Please, come in.

INT. ABBY'S HOUSE – DAY

*Abby and Mimi have just finished coffee. A videotape is on the table
between them.*

                    MIMI
. . . and I hadn't looked at it since then. But I was looking up
a speech I'd given and there it was. I remembered the review
for his play was in the Chicago paper, so I checked their
archives, and . . . well. You probably don't even want to see it,
but I thought, since I had this business trip . . .

                    ABBY
Thank you.

                    MIMI
I'm sorry. He seemed like a very nice man.

She stands as if to leave. Abby suddenly reaches out.

                    ABBY
Would you watch it with me? If I watch it now I can put it
away.

                    MIMI
              (*not that she wants to*)
All right.

Abby takes the tape, goes over to the VCR, puts it in, turns on the TV.

TV SCREEN

We see the moments in the bar hours before Greg dies. Laughing, shouting. He comes on the screen. He shows his wedding ring. He's happy.

ON ABBY

... who watches, pain written on her face. And now something else – shock.

BACK TO TV SCREEN

... which now shows Buddy:

>   BUDDY
>   (*on the tape*)
>   And Abby, whoever you are, forgive him, he did it for you.

On the tape we hear a boarding announcement for Flight 82.

>   (*on the tape*)
>   Ooops. That's me.

BACK TO SCENE

>   MIMI
>   That's a guy I was with. I never got his last name. We were
>   drinking. Cute, isn't he?

>   ABBY
>   What did he mean, 'He did it for you.'

>   MIMI
>   Your husband took a bump so he'd get this trip to Mexico
>   for you. And then, just at the last minute, this guy gave him
>   his seat so he could stay overnight . . .
>   (*weakly*)
>   We were flirting. Stupid.

>   ABBY
>   Fate, right?

                    MIMI

Yeah, I guess. Are you okay?

                    ABBY

I'm fine.

                    MIMI

Was it the right thing, bringing it?

                    ABBY

Yes, thank you.

They stand. Abby walks her to the door.

                    MIMI

Well . . .

                    ABBY

Thank you, Mimi.

Mimi nods, then goes. Abby closes the door. She goes back to the TV.

TV SCREEN

A freeze frame of Greg and Buddy.

EXT. ABBY'S HOUSE – DAY

After work. Buddy drives up, gets out.

INT. ABBY'S HOUSE – DAY

Joey's watching TV when Buddy knocks, enters. Darth (formerly Buddy) pounces on him.

                    BUDDY

Hey, Joey. Down, Darth, down.

                    JOEY

Hey, Mr. Amaral.

                    BUDDY

Abby!

          (*to Joey*)

Where's your mom?

                              JOEY
She's in the bathroom. She's been in there since *Rosie*.

                              BUDDY
Jeez. Who was on *Rosie*?

                              JOEY
Dunno.

INT. HALLWAY – NIGHT

Buddy taps on the door.

                              BUDDY
Abby? You okay?

Scott shoulders past him on his way to the living room.

                              ABBY
                        (*from inside*)
I'll be out in a minute.

Buddy notices something about her tone, shrugs it off, goes back into:

INT. LIVING ROOM – NIGHT

Scott and Joey are fighting over the remote to the TV.

                              BUDDY
                    (*on his way to the kitchen*)
Hey, hey, your mom's trying to relax.

                              JOEY
I was watching.

                              SCOTT
                (*re: a Hollywood Video tape on the floor*)
I gotta watch that, it's due tonight!

Joey kicks Scott and when Scott reacts, grabs the remote away from him. The VCR turns on. Scott pounces on Joey. Buddy intervenes, pulls Scott aside.

                              BUDDY
Hey, Scott. Don't hit him.

SCOTT
He bit me.

BUDDY
He's younger than you are. Joey, say you're sorry.

But Joey's looking at the screen. The volume's down low, but he's transfixed. Buddy looks from him to the TV.

TV SCREEN

Greg is there, laughing and smiling.

BACK TO SCENE

SCOTT
That's Dad!

JOEY
Hey, it's you!

– because Buddy is now on the screen. Buddy watches frozen. Suddenly, he jumps up, pushes eject, grabs the tape. Joey starts yelling.

Hey! That's my dad! I want to see it!

Scott is smarter.

SCOTT
Did you know my dad? When was that taken?

BUDDY
I knew him a little. I . . . just once. We had . . .

He sees they are both looking past him. He turns to see Abby in the doorway in her robe. One look at her expression confirms she's seen the tape.

. . . a drink once.

ABBY
Boys, go to your rooms until I call you.

SCOTT
I have to watch this tape –

ABBY

Scott. Please.

Scott takes Joey out of the room. Abby waits until the door closes. A beat, then:

BUDDY

Who gave you this?

ABBY

Mimi. Mimi Praeger. Remember her?

BUDDY

Yeah. Abby, I . . . I've been wanting to tell you. That's the thing I said I was gonna tell you.

ABBY

That's a lie. Another lie.

BUDDY

I felt responsible. He took my place. And I wanted to make sure you were okay, you and the kids.

ABBY

Who the hell do you think you are? God? Some fucking angel, come to make sure the victims are alive and well? You lied to me.

BUDDY

I didn't expect to fall in love with you.

ABBY

Liar. Liar –

BUDDY

No, you know that's true –

ABBY

I want you out of this house. I don't want to talk to you again. I don't want you to call. I don't want to hear your voice on my machine.

BUDDY

Give me a chance to explain.

ABBY

Didn't you hear me? Get out.

BUDDY

Abby –

ABBY

You son of a bitch. You lied to me. Get out!

Scott appears in the doorway.

SCOTT

Mom? What's wrong?

ABBY

Do you want me to say what you did in front of them? Because I'll do almost anything to get you out of here.

SCOTT

You better go, Mr. Amaral.

Buddy looks at Scott. He nods.

BUDDY

Okay, Scott. I think you're right.
   (*to Abby*)
I'll call you.

ABBY

Joey!
   (*to Buddy*)
Say good-bye to them. I don't want a guy just disappearing from their lives again.

Joey shows up at the doorway next to Scott.

Mr. Amaral won't be coming around anymore.

BUDDY

Abby, please.

ABBY

You can leave, or you can say good-bye and leave.

Buddy takes a moment to think about it. He squats down on Joey's level.

BUDDY
I gotta go away. But I hope someday I can come back.

JOEY
Why?

BUDDY
I kept a secret from your mother.

JOEY
You can't tell a secret.

BUDDY
Then it wasn't a secret. It was just something I didn't want to tell her.

JOEY
Say you're sorry.

BUDDY
I am sorry, but . . .

SCOTT
It's okay, Joey.

Buddy straightens up, looks at Abby.

BUDDY
You have to let me call you.

ABBY
Get out. Before I tell them who you are.

BUDDY
Abby, please –

ABBY
Just stay away from us, okay? Do us the favor you didn't do Greg.

Buddy goes white. A beat, then he leaves.

JOEY
Dad's on TV, Mom.

SCOTT

She knows, you idiot.

INT. BUDDY'S CONDO – DAY (DAWN)

Buddy looks like shit. He's been up all night trying to phone Abby. Finally he gets the announcement that the number has been changed and no new number is available.

INT. RESTAURANT – DAY

Abby and her lawyer, Ben Mandel, have just finished lunch.

MANDEL

I didn't know, Abby. I had no idea he was supposed to be on that flight.

ABBY

Okay. I had to ask. I thought you were friends.

MANDEL

Business.
(*beat*)
You say the employee at the gate knew they were switching?

ABBY

According to what Buddy told this woman. I don't want to talk about it anymore. You asked me why I was upset, I told you. Let me just sign the offer.

Mandel picks up the documents that were lying between them.

MANDEL

No, no, this is just a draft. I'll call you when the final comes in.

ABBY

Then why – oh, for God's sake.
(*standing up*)
I'm sorry, I'm grateful, Ben, really. You got us twice what they offered and that's going to help us get the hell out of here, move back home to Portland. But wrap it up quickly, okay? Thanks for lunch.

She leaves. Then he flips out his cell phone, makes a phone call.

> MANDEL
> (*into phone*)
> Annie? Get me Travis at Infinity. Tell him I need some of their personnel files.

INT. TANG-WELLER (TANG 2) – JIM'S OFFICE – DAY

Buddy enters, looking bad but not as bad as he will in a minute:

> BUDDY
> Jim? Seth says you wanted to see me?

He notices a lawyerly type, FRANK STEADMAN, sitting on the couch.

> Hey, Frank. We being sued or something?
> (*to Jim*)
> What's going on?

> JIM
> We received a call this morning from Vince Gardia . . .

> BUDDY
> And . . .

> JIM
> Infinity Air, according to its marketing vp, is deciding today whether they'll be requiring our services in the future.

> BUDDY
> What? Why?

> FRANK
> Apparently they've received information that you coerced an Infinity employee to illegally board a passenger under your name onto Flight 82. You remember Flight 82? It's substantiated by their roster, which shows you listed on that flight.

> BUDDY
> We sorted that out a year ago, right after the accident. Some computer problem. There's a correct version of the roster in their system somewhere.

FRANK

Yes, there is. Do you know a Janice Guerrero?

BUDDY

I don't think so.

FRANK

She was fired six weeks after the accident for altering the flight roster. Removing your name, in fact, and adding the name of a –

BUDDY

(*to prevent Jim from hearing his realtor's last name*)
What's all this got to do with their account with us?

JIM

There's a suit against Infinity brought by the victims' families. You know Ben Mandel? He's got a piece of it. Anyway, they want to prove the airline didn't follow procedures. Even technicalities. So Infinity wants to make sure that if you are called to testify, you'll tell the court what you told us. That you didn't persuade this gate attendant to board you. Because if you don't, Infinity closes their account with us, we don't get acquired by Koerner, and nobody in this room gets rich.

Buddy thinks. Fuck.

BUDDY

But this woman's going to testify.

FRANK

Maybe. But she's not the most credible witness. Bitter ex-employee, ax to grind. Infinity's position is the roster screw-up's a harmless computer glitch, no big deal. And they want to know if you'd have a problem with that?

BUDDY

No. No problem.

FRANK

Good. You can expect to be subpoenaed. Naturally, we'll be your counsel. Jim.

He leaves. Jim, worried, watches Buddy.

JIM
That fucking crash, huh?

Buddy nods, tries to smile . . .

EXT. JANELLO HOUSE – STREET – DAY

Buddy has pulled up outside of Abby's house. He's got to see her. He takes a breath, gets out of his car, heads to the front door – and Scott comes out. Buddy stops. Scott comes toward him.

SCOTT
She's not home. Even if she was . . .

BUDDY
She doesn't want to see me.

SCOTT
Yeah.

BUDDY
I figured. Did she explain to you why she's mad at me?

SCOTT
You were with my dad in the airport and didn't tell her.

BUDDY
I wouldn't blame you if you were mad at me, too.

SCOTT
It's okay.

BUDDY
Okay. Good. Well, I guess I –

SCOTT
Did he say anything about Christmas trees?

BUDDY
What?

SCOTT
My dad. He was supposed to sell Christmas trees with me the next day. Maybe that's why he tried to get back on the plane that crashed. So I was wondering if he said anything about that.

Buddy has a chance to tell the truth. This isn't the time.

BUDDY
He didn't mention that to me. He just wanted to get back home as soon as he could. Everybody does when they're at the airport.

SCOTT
Because I didn't care if he sold those trees with me. I didn't want to, even. Everybody has fake ones anyway.

BUDDY
He said he had to get back home to work. I remember that. Nothing about the trees.

Something inside Scott eases, maybe for the first time since the accident.

SCOTT
Okay. Do you think I should tell my mom? Because maybe she thinks it's 'cause she yelled at him. Over the tree thing.

BUDDY
She might not believe me.
         (not for his own sake)
You believe me, though, right?

SCOTT
Yeah.

BUDDY
Good. Joey okay?

SCOTT
Yeah. He's gonna forget you, you know. He practically doesn't remember Dad but I'm not allowed to say that to him anymore.

BUDDY
Yeah, well. You don't have to tell your mom I stopped by if you don't want.

SCOTT
I might leave it out. Just . . . I better.

                           BUDDY
    Okay. Well. See ya.

Scott gives him a little two-fingered salute, just like Greg did on page 12.

                           SCOTT
    Later.

This stops Buddy, but he smiles, goes to his car. Watches Scott staring at him as he leaves.

EXT. BUDDY'S CONDO BUILDING – NIGHT

Buddy comes home with a bag of groceries. Seth is at his front door.

                           SETH
    You forgot your ticket.

INT. BUDDY'S CONDO – NIGHT

Buddy's putting the groceries away; Seth is flipping through a folder.

                           SETH
    You're in the same hotel as Jim. He touched down about an
    hour ago with Frank.

                           BUDDY
    Okay, great.

                           SETH
    Phone list. Production estimate came in at five-three-zero.
    Josh says he'll handle the client call unless you want to take
    the heat. Everything else can wait. Oh, Ben Mandel called.
    'Sorry about the subpoena.'

                           BUDDY
    It's not his fault. And Abby . . . I guess you can't blame her
    for getting even.

                           SETH
    She's not his client anymore. She settled. It was in the
    papers. Mandel glommed onto some other families.

BUDDY

She shouldn't have settled.

SETH

Yeah, why don't you call her? I'm sure she'd like your take on it.

BUDDY

You had dinner?

SETH

Are you asking me to dinner?

BUDDY

I'm asking if you had it.

SETH

Actually I've got plans with Adam. You want to come along? We'll sit you between us and you can pretend you're in prison.

Unthinkingly, Buddy takes out a liquor bottle from the Vendome bag. It's unopened, but . . .

What's that?

BUDDY

Oh come on, Seth. What are you going to do, give me a lecture? Give me a break, the world's not exactly my fucking oyster lately.

SETH

Don't let me stop you. In fact . . .
    (*sliding a glass over to Buddy*)
It's not like it's part of my job to keep you sober.

BUDDY

You got that right.

SETH

Just like it's not your job to not disappoint me. Knock yourself out, man.

He leaves. Buddy looks at the bottle.

INT. O'HARE AIRPORT – INFINITY GATE AREA – DAY

Late afternoon. Buddy exits the plane and sees the airport bar...

INT. O'HARE – INFINITY GATE AREA – BAR – DAY

Buddy looks at the cocktail table he, Greg, and Mimi shared a year and a half ago. For a brief moment, he sees Mimi and Greg – and himself – looking at him expectantly. He closes his eyes, opens them again. They're gone.

INT. CHICAGO HOTEL – DAY

Buddy's on the phone.

                    BUDDY
    Oh, okay, fine. Jim, come on, go ahead and have dinner with
    them, I'm fine. Just don't tell me what you guys talk about,
    that'd be collusion. That's a joke. Call me when you get in.
    Room two-thirty-three.

He hangs up, flips on the news.

TV SCREEN – LOCAL NEWS

Too blonde, too many teeth, a reporter at the news desk with a blue-screen window behind her:

                    REPORTER
    ... earlier today in Kansas ...

They roll some tape: a stone marker is unveiled ...

    ... commemorating the two hundred and sixteen deaths on
    Infinity Flight 82 nearly eighteen months ago. Since then,
    Infinity, which began life as a commuter airline in 1979, has
    been plagued by lawsuits. Still, the upstart airline has suc-
    cessfully settled all but three of the lawsuits pending in the
    case, and its stock last week returned to its pre-crash levels
    for the first time. Wall Street's keeping an eye on the only
    case to reach the courts so far, which today entered its sec-
    ond week. The families of passengers Chris Hogan and
    Eloise Langan –

BACK TO SCENE

Buddy flips the channel to something innocuous.

INT. HOTEL COFFEE SHOP – NIGHT

Apparently Jim never called Buddy back. Buddy enters the hotel coffee shop near closing time – and sees Janice Guerrero at a table near the back. Buddy looks around, sees that no one is watching.

BUDDY

Janice?

Janice looks up at him. She's angry, and her eyes have dark circles under them.

JANICE

Oh. It's you. They called you.

BUDDY

You, too?

JANICE

Are you kidding? I'm an example of the sloppy, dollars-first attitude of Infinity. The plaintiffs love me – even though what they're saying is I killed their families.

BUDDY

You didn't kill anybody.

JANICE

Yeah, I've mentioned that. And they say if I'd done my job, that plane wouldn't have taken off.

BUDDY

No –

JANICE

Hey, I remember what happened. Don't you?

FLASHBACK: INT. O'HARE – NIGHT

Buddy and Janice are talking confidentially.

JANICE
I can't board him under your name.
(*to Buddy*)
Are you worried about the weather? It's just snow.

BUDDY
Janice, come on. If I don't board, you'll have to delay the flight until they take my bags off. This way . . . we just switch. You guys leave on time. It's fine. You want another half-hour delay?

JANICE
So I just didn't recognize you.

BUDDY
That's right. You never saw me.

JANICE
You owe me.

BUDDY
I'm back here next week.

BACK TO SCENE (PRESENT TIME)

BUDDY
I should have been on that flight. I should be dead right now.

JANICE
Yeah, you should. Or at least just too fucking ashamed to come near me.

BUDDY
Janice, you –

JANICE
You could've called me, Buddy. You could have called me once since the crash.

BUDDY
I didn't want to – I thought I was doing you a favor staying away.

JANICE

Oh yeah, Mr. Big Guy, always doing people favors, always making everything come out right. You think I'm so stupid I don't know it's all about you? You think everyone you do one of your favors for is that stupid?

She stands up and leaves.

EXT. COURTHOUSE – DAY

Big crowds, cameras, reporters ... Buddy and Frank Steadman, Tang-Weller's lawyer, pass a family member holding a photo sign: it's of Ron Wachter, the man Buddy talked to (see page 5). It stops Buddy when he sees it; then he goes inside.

INT. CORRIDOR – DAY

Frank and Buddy show his subpoena to a BAILIFF, who shepherds them through the press stationed outside the courtroom. WE STAY ON A COURT TV REPORTER who's filing a live report.

TV REPORTER

Holly, Bill, I would say that was devastating testimony – for those of you joining us this is day seven of the civil suit against Infinity Airlines, and believe me, the tensions which have been running high since the suit began are likely to reach their peak today ...

INT. CORRIDOR – WITNESS HOLDING AREA – DAY

Buddy takes a seat on some benches in the hallway with the other witnesses. Frank's on his cell phone.

BUDDY'S POV – OTHER WITNESSES

A group of families are sitting together. It's obvious from their red-rimmed eyes they're the bereaved.

TV REPORTER (V.O.)

– the plaintiffs are the survivors of three passengers, two of whom, ironically, were seated across the aisle from each other, in seats 18B and 18C ...

Buddy sees a commotion at the door to the courtroom. Suddenly cameras are snapping as Janice Guerrero exits the courtroom.

> And Holly, here's today's principal witness, whose testimony about the boarding of Flight 82 exposed a disregard of safety that was extremely damaging to Infinity's case. Let's see if we can speak to her. Janice! Janice, please, are you sorry for what you did –

TV SCREEN

. . . with a COURT TV *logo on it. Janice is being pushed through the crowd by her attorney. She shakes her head. 'No comment,' says her lawyer.*

INT. ABBY'S HOUSE – KITCHEN – DAY

Abby's watching this on TV, riveted. In the month since we've seen her, she's taken up smoking again and called in sick most Mondays.

INT. COURTROOM – DAY

Buddy is led in by the bailiff to the expectant court. Frank whispers a few words in his ear, then sits in one of the rows in the back, next to Jim. At the plaintiff's table sits Ben Mandel with two co-counsels. As he sits down on the stand, Buddy looks at the families. As he's sworn in – by the name of Robert Amaral – he sees Jim, who nods at Buddy, a 'you-know-what-you-need-to-do' nod. Buddy nods back.

> BUDDY
> (*taking the oath*)
> Yes, I do.

> MANDEL
> (*rising*)
> Your Honor, this witness is affiliated with the defendant. We would like to treat him as a hostile witness.

> JUDGE
> Any objection? Proceed.

> MANDEL
> Mr. Amaral, you were scheduled to be a passenger on Flight 82, were you not?

BUDDY
Yes, I was.

MANDEL
In fact, when the plane went down, your name was on the first list of passengers, was it not?

BUDDY
That's correct.

MANDEL
But instead, a Mr. Greg Janello was in your seat, isn't that correct?

BUDDY
I believe so, yes.

MANDEL
You believe so?

BUDDY
I mean, yes, he was in my seat.

MANDEL
Do you know how Mr. Janello happened to be on that plane occupying your seat?

BUDDY
No, I uh . . . I don't know.

MANDEL
Excuse me?

BUDDY
I don't . . . I'm very confused about what happened that night.

MANDEL
You're not confused about having just taken an oath to tell the truth, are you?

INFINITY ATTORNEY
Objection, Your Honor. Badgering the witness.

MANDEL

I'll rephrase, Your Honor. Mr. Amaral, did you have a conversation that night with Mr. Janello?

BUDDY

I had a lot of conversations with a lot of people. Everything was delayed. It was a long time ago.

MANDEL

This is Mr. Janello.

Mandel holds up a picture of Greg Janello – half of the Greg–Abby photo Buddy saw in Greg's home office. Buddy stares at it, uncomfortable. He looks up, catches Jim and Frank watching him. He looks over at the Infinity lawyers.

Did you have a conversation with this man?

BUDDY

Yes.

MANDEL

And did you offer to switch boarding passes with him?

BUDDY
(*he looks at Jim, then*)

No.

Jim breathes out with relief. Then:

I just gave him mine. I didn't take his.

MANDEL

And when Ms. Guerrero recognized you at the gate?

BUDDY

I talked her into it.

MANDEL

By telling her if they didn't board you, or someone claiming to be you, they'd have to wait while they took your luggage out of the hold.

BUDDY

Basically, yeah.

MANDEL
Are you aware that airlines have to deplane the luggage of passengers who don't make the flight as an antiterrorism measure?

BUDDY
Yeah, in case someone checks a bomb or something and then doesn't get on the plane.

MANDEL
It's for safety, in other words.

BUDDY
Yes.

MANDEL
So this employee of Infinity disregarded a safety measure due to her desire to make the schedule.

INFINITY ATTORNEY
Objection! Argumentative!

JUDGE
Sustained –

BUDDY
– She just wanted to do me a favor.

MANDEL
No one's blaming you, Mr. Amaral. It wasn't your job to make sure the airline followed its own safety procedures, was it? No further questions –

BUDDY
He was scared, you know. I didn't remember that till later.

MANDEL
Excuse me?

INT. AIRPORT – NIGHT (FLASHBACK)

Buddy and Greg in line at the Infinity gate.

GREG
You're not scared of flying, are you?

BUDDY
I'd rather be on a plane than anywhere. Safer than cars, you know.

GREG
You don't have any kids. They make cowards of you, children.

BUDDY
It's like a boat on the water.

GREG
Yeah, and boats never sink? 'I know that I shall meet my fate/Somewhere among the clouds above.' You know that one? Yeats.

BUDDY
Not the dooryard guy again.

GREG
'An Irish Airman Foresees His Death.'

BUDDY
Kind of explains why I haven't run across it in the in-flight magazine.

GREG
This guy's this aristocrat. He guards people who can't be helped, and he fights people he doesn't hate, and since nothing means anything, why not live recklessly, you know? Bold guy, gambler. And I used to think when I was a kid, that's what you should shoot for. But instead I worry about cancer and drive-bys and bombs and de-icing.

BUDDY
Hey, when your number's up . . .

GREG
You gonna sleep with her?

BUDDY
Why not?

GREG

See, you got it. That whole 'what me worry?' thing. I admire that.

BACK TO SCENE IN COURTROOM

BUDDY

But he was lying. He didn't admire it. He saw right through me. He knew I didn't care about shit, and that he did, and he had a wife and kids and a life that mattered, so much that he was scared of flying, and I had nothing and I thought for a second, Fuck you, pal.

Buddy's finally going to admit what he hasn't been able to till now.

I didn't know the plane was going to go down, okay? But I had this thought, which was, I hope you get four hours of turbulence, man, and maybe a tiny little sudden loss of altitude, and maybe you shit in your pants a little. Because he had what even I knew I wasn't ever going to have, and he knew it. And you don't wish those kind of people well. And then he died. And that's what I gotta carry.

There's a silence in the courtroom.

MANDEL

No further questions, Your Honor.

BUDDY

I'd just like to say I'm sorry.

But no one seems to be listening.

INFINITY ATTORNEY

No cross.

JUDGE

You're excused, Mr. Amaral.

BUDDY

Am I? Excused?

He smiles. 'Excused.' He gets out, walks out of the courtroom, past Frank's and the Infinity team's stony looks. Jim watches him, saddened.

INT. JANELLO HOUSE – KITCHEN – DAY

Abby watches this on the television, tears in her eyes. For Greg. And maybe for Buddy.

INT. BUDDY'S CHICAGO HOTEL ROOM – NIGHT

Buddy, packing, watching a wrap-up of the trial. In a surprise move, Infinity settled big with the plaintiffs – without admitting fault. We hold on him a moment, utterly defeated, down to zero. And yet, this is the first time he looks at peace. On the bed beside him is a paperback copy of Leaves of Grass *by Walt Whitman – Greg's 'dooryard guy'…*

FADE OUT.

FADE IN:

INT. TANG-WELLER (TANG 2) – BUDDY'S OFFICE – DAY

Buddy enters. Seth is there.

> SETH
> The word is you pretty much single-handedly sank Infinity.

> BUDDY
> Yeah, I noticed a chill on the way in.

> SETH
> Well, bundle up. Jim wants to see you.

> BUDDY
> Type this up for me, would you?

He hands Seth a letter. Seth reads it, looks up in surprise.

INT. JIM'S OFFICE – DAY

Jim is reading the now freshly typed resignation letter.

> JIM
> I'm not accepting this. Infinity can hardly fire us because one of our team didn't commit perjury. Anyway, now they need us to handle the fallout from this settlement. Let's just sit tight.

BUDDY

Oh, they'll keep us on – but only if I go. They're waiting for you to make the move. Come on. It's for the best.

JIM

I won't let you resign.

BUDDY

Then fire me. Infinity likes that hardball stuff.

JIM

You're my friend. I'm not going to fire you.

Buddy takes a breath. He wishes he didn't have to say this:

BUDDY

You know the broker who handled this building? Abby? She didn't find it. I told her about it. I threw her the sale. She was someone I'd been seeing. I cost this company $200,000. You don't need that, Jim. Fire me.

JIM

You lied to me?

BUDDY

Yeah. I'd do it again.

JIM

I wish you hadn't told me that, Buddy. I'd've fired you in a week or so anyway.

BUDDY
(*not believing him*)
Yeah, right, Jim. That's you. Take care.

He turns and leaves. Jim looks at the letter again, places it carefully in his 'In' box.

INT. BUDDY'S OFFICE – NIGHT

Seth and Buddy are boxing up his office.

INT. BUDDY'S CONDO – DAY

Buddy stares into space.

INT. SETH'S APARTMENT – NIGHT

Seth and his boyfriend ADAM are making dinner. Buddy sits on a stool in the kitchen, watching.

SETH

I almost quit after you did. Then I thought, Shit, I don't even like the guy.

ADAM

Yeah, right.
(*to Buddy*)
You guys had me worried there for a while. The whole boss–secretary thing.

SETH

Hey. Boss–*assistant*.
(*to Adam*)
Look at him watching us. Like he's about to ask which one's the husband and which one's the wife.

BUDDY

You'll tell me when you're ready.

ADAM

Good. Then you can tell me.

SETH

How was the meeting?

BUDDY

Typical. Isn't it great we're not drinking? Incidentally, God rules.

SETH

Yeah, what's a nice guy like you doing in a place like that? Oh yeah, you're a fucking drunk.

ADAM

You know, we're thinking of a regional campaign where I work. We do interactive design, websites. It'd be mostly print and radio, but I could get you a meeting.

BUDDY

Hey, sure. Appreciate it.

SETH

Hand me that, would you?

He indicates a colander over by the wall phone. As Buddy reaches for it, he sees a calendar. On the calendar, next Saturday is circled with the word Abby. *Buddy looks at Seth.*

BUDDY

Is that Abby Janello?

SETH

Yeah. We got kind of friendly there while you were . . . whatever that was.

BUDDY

She ever mention me?

SETH

You want me to find out if she'll say yes if you ask her to the dance? Grow up, man. The boys survived, if you're interested. You want to eat or not?

He and Adam put dinner on the table. Buddy still has his eye on the calendar.

EXT. ROOFTOP PARKING LOT – DAY

Late afternoon. Adam walks Buddy toward his car.

ADAM

That went well. He's not the easiest guy in the world.

BUDDY

I know the type. I was the type. Look, I can do mock-ups of what we talked about in two weeks. I gotta sub some of it out, but –

ADAM

Give us a proposal first. Bare bones, okay?

BUDDY

Yeah, sure. Thanks, Adam.

Adam hands him parking stickers. As Buddy sticks them on:

Listen, uh . . . when you guys see Abby tonight, would you mind just mentioning that I –

ADAM
Tonight? Oh, the calendar thing. That was for Seth. He went over there this morning to help her pack up.

BUDDY
What –

ADAM
She's moving back home – Portland, I think. You didn't hear that from me.

BUDDY
When, today?

ADAM
In fact, he and her friend, they're taking them to the airport now.

BUDDY
Shit.

ADAM
(*after a beat*)
Nine-thirty. LAX. You didn't hear that from me, too.

BUDDY
Thanks, Adam –

ADAM
Hey, Buddy? Seth likes the cheap lots.

EXT. LAX – PARKING LOT C – NIGHT

Buddy pulls into the remote parking lot and drives down the aisles, looking for Abby and Seth. He sees them, and Donna, behind him, but now a shuttle bus and car are blocking him. He gets out of the car, starts running, calling Abby's name.

ABBY, SETH, AND DONNA

... are pushing some trolleys loaded with luggage. Joey and Scott are ahead of them. Abby hears Buddy shouting her name. She turns, sees him, then looks at Donna.

DONNA

I didn't tell him.

SETH

Fuck. Adam.

BUDDY

Abby! Abby!

Now Scott and Joey have stopped, are looking back at Abby, Seth, and Donna – and beyond them, Buddy.

ABBY
(*to Scott and Joey*)

Go on, keep going.

SETH

He'll just get on the plane. He'll be puking with fear, but it's possible. I'll wait with the boys.

ABBY

No, wait, wait –

DONNA

You want me to stay, I'll stay.
(*a look at her, then to Joey and Scott*)
Guys! Wait up!

They leave with the luggage. Abby breathes in, turns to face Buddy, who arrives panting, his face damp with sweat.

BUDDY

Thank you. Thanks.

He's out of breath. He leans against a nearby car.

ABBY

Are you all right?

BUDDY
Yeah, yeah. I . . . you look . . . beautiful.

ABBY
It's the jet exhaust. Filters the light. Well. We're leaving for Portland.

BUDDY
I know. Adam told . . . I didn't hear it from Adam.

ABBY
I didn't want to see you again.

BUDDY
I know, I don't blame you –

ABBY
But I did. On TV. At the trial. I heard what you said about Greg.

BUDDY
I don't know why I said that –

ABBY
Maybe because it was true. Unless that's not a reason for you.

BUDDY
No, it is. Abby, I just –

ABBY
Hey. I got a marriage proposal. From Steve – Greg's old partner, remember him? He came over one night a month after Sue had the baby. I kicked him out and he called the next day and said it was the postpartum depression, and I said, She'll snap out of it, and he said, No, *my* postpartum depression.
(*beat; this kills her:*)
I don't want to hear anything from you, Buddy. I just don't because it's no good.

BUDDY
I don't expect you to forgive me. I don't deserve it. But who deserves anything they get, you know? You didn't deserve

what you got, or the boys, or Greg. So maybe being forgiven will be what I get and don't deserve.

ABBY

I've forgiven you, Buddy.

BUDDY

I thought maybe we could talk someday. That's what was in my letters. Maybe today's not good, or soon, but . . .
(he can't finish; simply:)
I want to see you, Abby. Not seeing you is harder than anything.
(trying to joke)
You know what that does to a person. Makes you irritable.

ABBY

Yeah, I miss you, Buddy, and I miss him, and sometimes I can't tell the two feelings apart. And it makes me so angry. Let me ask you something, and if you lie to me I'll know. Are you sorry you didn't get on that plane?

BUDDY

(after a beat)
No. I'm sorry, but I'm glad I'm alive.

ABBY

And nobody blames you for that. But ask *me* the question. Am I sorry you didn't get on the plane? Whatever I answer, yes or no, it feels like I'm doing something wrong to someone I . . . to both of you, you and Greg. Being with you is like making a choice.

BUDDY

You don't have that choice, about whether he lives or dies. Neither do I. We've got other choices.

ABBY

What am I supposed to do? Pretend we've never met before? You never met Greg, you weren't the one who –

BUDDY

No, I'm the guy who *lived* instead of him. That's who you'd be talking to.

Inside Abby something clicks into place. She looks at him and quietly makes her choice. While Buddy waits to be told, an airplane makes a deafening noise from the nearby runway as it prepares for takeoff. She turns to look at it. So does he.

> ABBY
>
> This is the scary part. Now, right before it takes off. Because it just seems so . . . unlikely.
>
> BUDDY
>
> You're not scared of flying.
>
> ABBY
>
> I'm not talking about flying.

She looks at him, and then again at the plane approaching. Together they stand together and watch the plane coming closer and then lifting away from the ground, toward them, and over their heads.

From behind we see them standing, looking up at the plane. Then Buddy reaches for her hand, and she lets him take it, that's all, and they still stand there, watching.

And then they turn, toward us, and Abby's smiling and brushing something from her face and raising her hand to wave to her kids, and Buddy picks up her bag, not letting her go, and then they're both past us and we're following behind them, and beyond them WE SEE Scott and Joey begin to walk and then run toward them and US, and just as they reach Abby and Buddy, WE GO UP and over them, and then OUT to the sky, where the plane is only lights now, among hundreds of lights, and we hang there a moment and then . . .

FADE OUT.

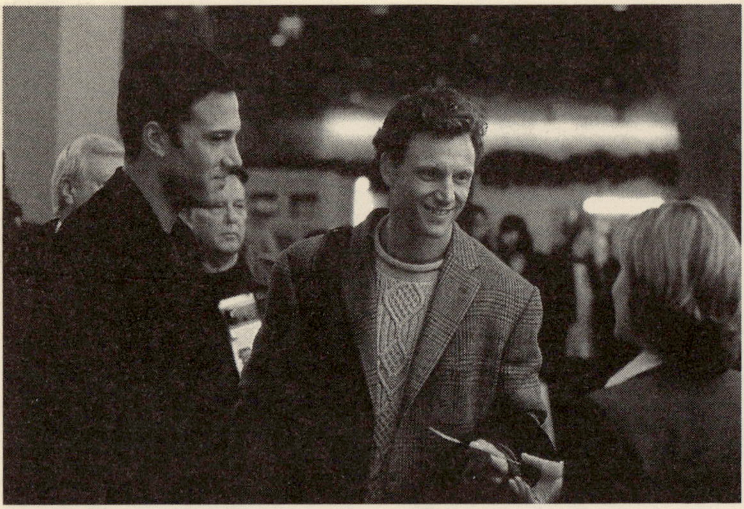

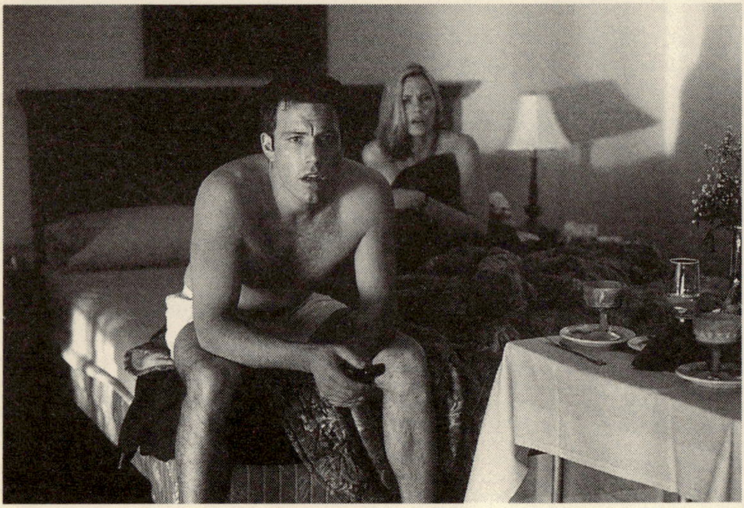

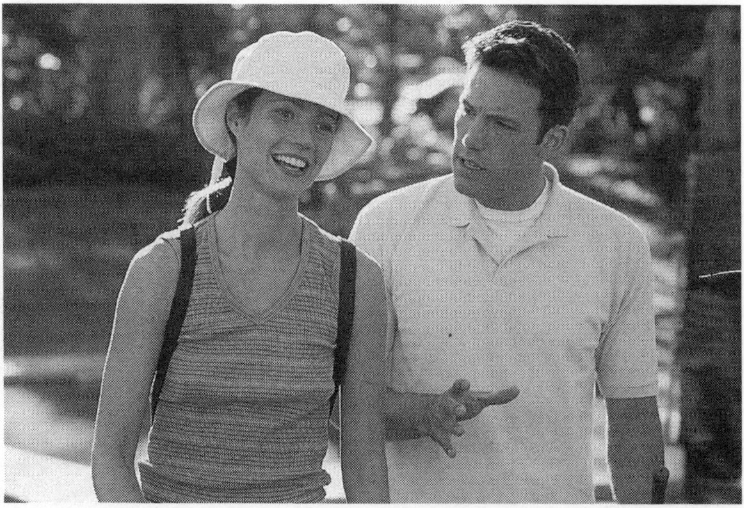

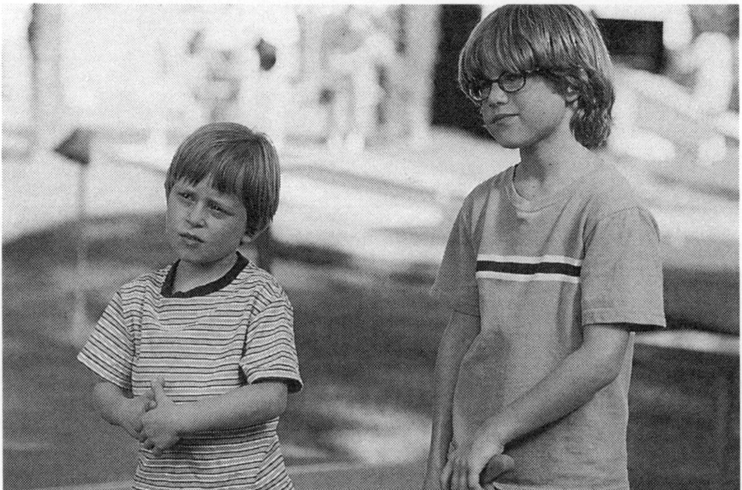

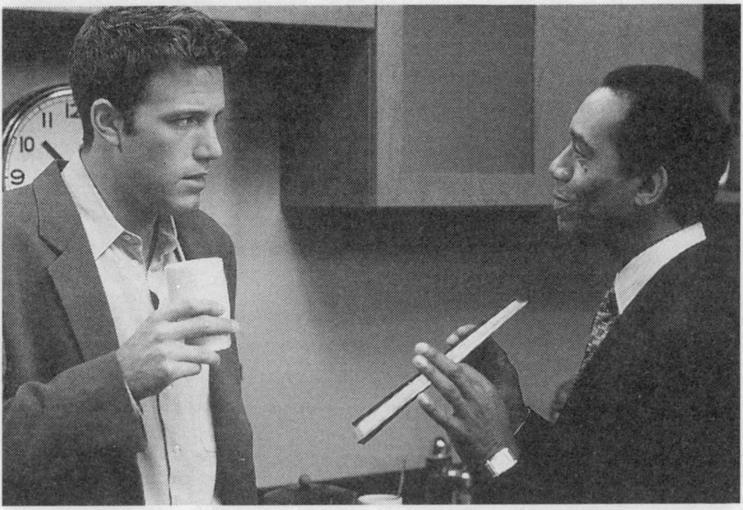
12
11
10
9

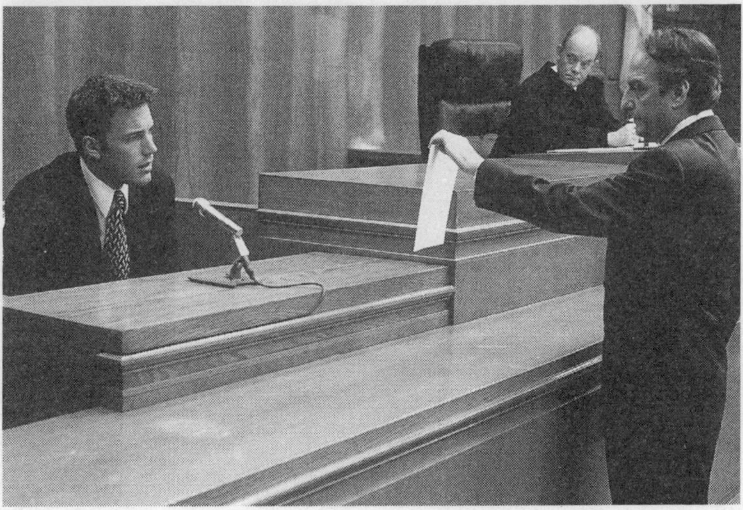

Ben Affleck and Gwyneth Paltrow with writer/director Don Roos

The Opposite of Sex

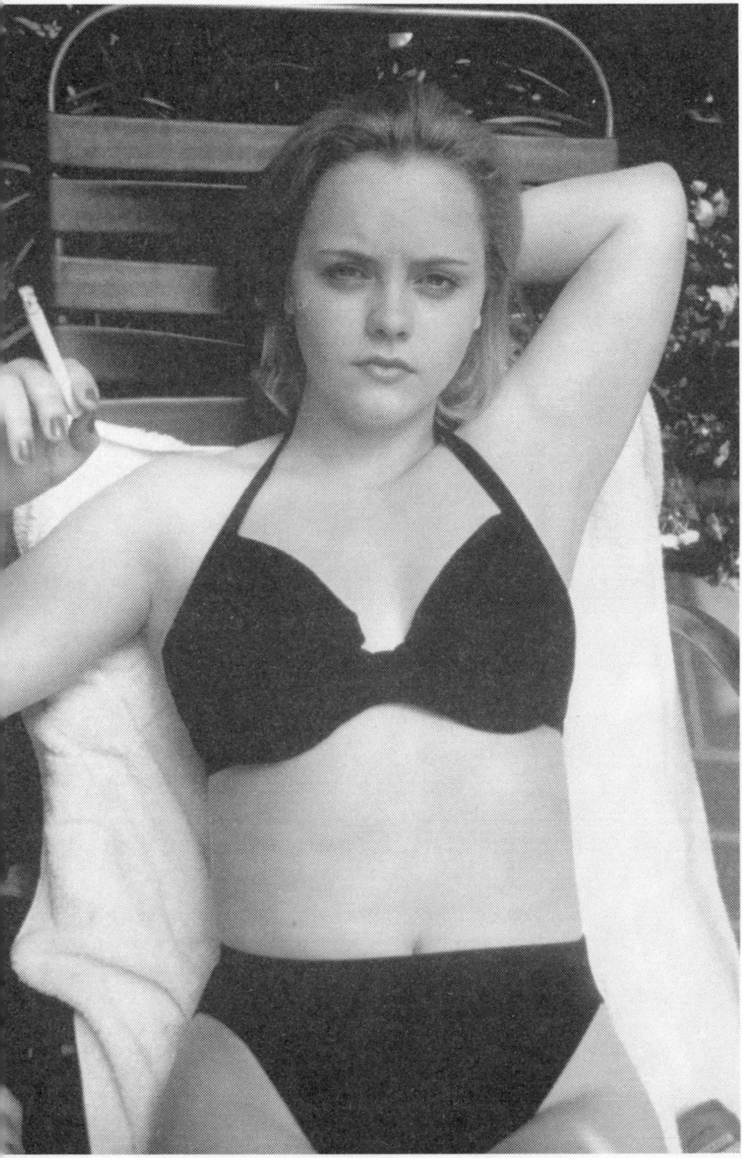

The Opposite of Sex was first released in the United States by Sony Pictures Classics in May 1998.

MAIN CAST

DEDEE TRUITT	Christina Ricci
BILL TRUITT	Martin Donovan
LUCIA DALURY	Lisa Kudrow
CARL TIPPETT	Lyle Lovett
JASON BOCK	Johnny Galecki
RANDY	William Lee Scott
MATT MATTEO	Ivan Sergei
BOBETTE KULP	Megan Blake
TOM DALURY	Colin Ferguson
TIMOTHY	Dan Bucatinsky

MAIN CREW

Directed by	Don Roos
Written by	Don Roos
Produced by	Michael Besman
	David Kirkpatrick
Executive Producers	Steve Danton
	Jim Lotfi
Original Music by	Mason Daring
Cinematography by	Hubert Taczanowski
Film Editing by	David Codron
Casting	Amanda Mackey Johnson
	Cathy Sandrich
Production Design by	Michael Clausen
Costume Design by	Peter Mitchell

FADE IN:
INT. DEDEE TRUITT'S HOUSE, NORTHERN LOUISIANA – DAY

BOBETTE KULP, a cat on her lap, is painting her nails in the living room of her run-down Louisiana home. A ring of car keys is thrown at her, startling the cat and ruining her nail job. She screams at her unseen daughter and struggles to her feet, and we FOLLOW HER for a moment as she reaches her daughter's bedroom door, yelling some more and then giving up.

WE PUSH PAST HER into the bedroom, where we glimpse the back of her daughter Dedee as she gets dressed. She's running around her small, untidy bedroom, struggling into a tight, low-cut dress.

DEDEE TRUITT is sixteen. Fifteen was her year of firsts: date, tattoo, blow-job – all on the same night. Now she's up to her third tattoo and her whatever blow-job, all before she's gotten to the Civil War in school. She comes out of the bathroom and studies herself in the wall mirror. She leans in to flick her nipples through the thin cloth of her dress. She frowns, then puts on sunglasses. She talks tough. For her, tough is the opposite of lonely, so she works at it.

> DEDEE (V.O.)
> If you're one of those people who don't like movies where some person you can't see talks the whole time and covers up all the holes in the plot and at the end says, 'I was never the same again after that summer,' or whatever, like it was so deep they can't stand it, then you're out of luck. Things get very complicated here very quick, and my guess is you're not gonna be up to it without me talking. My name is Dedee Truitt, I'm sixteen, and this is Crevecoeur, Louisiana, which is French I think for like, Fucked Heart.

EXT. CEMETERY – DAY

Dedee, in her tight dress and high heels, watches as a coffin is lowered into the ground.

Next to her is her mother, Bobette Kulp, trying her best to look like Jackie getting off Air Force One right after the coffin. Bobette reaches down, gently tosses a clump of dirt onto the lowering coffin. She turns to Dedee, whispers something to her. Dedee bends down, grabs a clump of clay, and hurls it into the grave. Then another clump, then a folding chair, then three vases of flowers. Her mother starts screaming, restrains her. No one is scandalized. These two have a reputation.

DEDEE (V.O.)
My stepfather was a real asshole. To get cancer of the ass was like, poetic. Almost as good as cancer of the dick, if they have that.

INT. DEDEE'S BEDROOM — NIGHT (M.O.S.)*

Dedee sits on her bed smoking; Bobette's in the doorway, drink and TV guide in hand. They have an unfriendly conversation till Bobette leaves. Dedee waits, then grabs a packed duffel from under the bed. One more thing: she goes to her night-stand and takes out a gun. She buries this in the duffel.

---

*M.O.S.: Without sound.

                        DEDEE (V.O.)
My mother was the kind of mother who always said she was
her daughter's best friend. Whenever she did I thought, great,
not only do I have a shitty mother but my best friend's a loser-
bitch. She was all over me the day we buried Les. She said she
was going to lean on me now that he was dead and her heart
was wore out. Believe me, if Les wore out anything of hers it
wasn't her heart. I had to get out of there. Oh, this part where
I take the gun is like, duh. Important. It comes back later but
I'm putting it here for foreshadowing, which we covered when
we did Dickens. If you're smart you won't forget I've got it.

EXT. KULP HOUSE, CREVECOEUR – NIGHT

*A seventeen-year-old boy, RANDY, is walking back to his car when the
front door of the house opens quietly and Dedee runs out. He's pissed;
Dedee's anxious to keep him quiet; she looks back at the house to make
sure they're not being watched. There's lightning out; a storm is coming.*

                        DEDEE (V.O.)
Randy was a geek, but he was nicer than a lot of the guys
mostly because he was born with only one ball, and he was
pretty nice to anyone who'd sleep with him and not make fun
of it. You had to ignore the Christian stuff.

EXT. NORTH SHREVEPORT BUS STATION – NIGHT (RAIN)

*Randy gives Dedee a silver cross on a chain. She smiles, trying not to
roll her eyes, then gives him a big kiss. She's standing in front of a
Houston bus, wants him to leave her there, waves him away. He doesn't
want to. She pushes him away, flips him the bird. Pissed off, he leaves.
She shoulders her backpack, walks towards a bus marked 'Chicago'.*

                        DEDEE (V.O.)
I told him I was going to my grandma's in Houston . . . but
where I was really going was Indiana to see my brother Bill,
who was really only my half-brother, and who I'd seen like
once before when I was a kid, when my real dad died. Bill's
like dozens of years older than me and an actual real-life
homo, and a teacher, which is kind of gross, I mean the
combo, but he had money from his last boyfriend, who died

of AIDS, natch, and I needed a place to get my shit together.

INT. BUS — (MOVING) — NIGHT

Dedee is sitting next to an old man who is snoring and leaning into her. She is using the silver cross to pick chewing gum off the seat in front of her. She elbows the old man sharply in the side, twice. He moves to another seat.

DEDEE (V.O.)
If you think I'm just plucky and scrappy and all I need is love, you're in over your head. I don't have a heart of gold and I don't grow one later, okay?

INT./EXT. PHONE BOOTH; SOUTH BEND, INDIANA — DAY

Dedee looks up an address in the phone book.

DEDEE (V.O.)
But relax, there's other people a lot nicer coming up. We call them losers.

EXT. NICE NEIGHBORHOOD, SOUTH BEND — DAY

Old homes, built for the Studebaker executives when the plant was in production. Sidewalks, tricycles, picket fences.

DEDEE (V.O.)
Look at this. It's the fucking City of Trikes.

EXT. BILL'S HOUSE — DAY

Dedee walks up the path to one of these homes, rings the bell. After a moment, a good-looking young man, no Einstein and no need to be, opens the door. This is MATT MATTEO. He's in workout clothes, well-used and sweaty. Hot.

MATT
Hello.

DEDEE
(*puzzled*)
You're not Bill . . .

MATT

I'm Matt. Bill's at school. Are you one of his students?
            (*friendly, conspiratorial*)
'Cause he doesn't really like his students coming here.

                    DEDEE

I'm his sister.

                    MATT

Oh.

Now he brings up the arm that's been hidden behind the door; we see he's on the phone.

            (*into phone*)
Call you back.
            (*he hangs up*)
I didn't know he had a sister.

                    DEDEE

Who are you?

                    MATT

Boyfriend.

Dedee's face is eloquent: Yuck.

                    DEDEE

Can I come in? I'm a real relation.

A school bell rings from the next scene.

INT. HOOVER HIGH SCHOOL MEN'S ROOM – DAY

BILL TRUITT enters. Mid-thirties, the still waters type. Maybe he's a pushover; maybe he just picks his fights. It's hard to tell looking at him what he likes in bed, or with whom, but you get the idea whatever he likes he likes a lot. Students are smoking and horsing around.

                    BILL

Hey. Butts out. Come on.

We hear the words 'Mr. Truitt.' The kids obey, even if slowly. One of them mutters, 'Asshole.' One boy stays behind, leaning against the wall. Bill notices he's got a pen in his hand. The kid's name is JOE.

Joe? You holding up that wall?

JOE
It's just . . . I can't go if anyone's around.

Bill has noticed the pen in Joe's hand. He looks at Joe, who moves aside reluctantly. Bill squints at the adolescent graffiti on the wall. It reads, MR. TRUITT SUCKS IT HARD. EVERY TUESDAY AFTER YEARBOOK HERE. *Bill looks at this a long moment. He knows what the world's capable of calamity-wise, and this isn't close. Joe won't meet his eyes.*

BILL
There's a sentence here that's a fragment. What is it?

Joe is scared this is a trick.

'Every . . .'

JOE
'Every Tuesday after yearbook here.'

BILL
How would you take care of that?

JOE
Well, you could say, 'Mr. Truitt . . . you know, blanks it hard here every Tuesday after yearbook.'

BILL
Or just 'Tuesdays after yearbook.' You don't need the 'every'. Right?

JOE
Yeah, I guess so. Can I go?

He hands Bill the pen; before he leaves, Bill makes him flush the urinal. After he's gone, Bill sees some more graffiti – a line drawing of a naked woman. He tries rubbing it off; it doesn't rub off. He uses his pen to turn it into a picture of a bearded man. When he steps back to admire it, he sees another kid, TY, reading the first graffiti – and seeing Bill with the green pen in his hand.

TY
It's probably not a good idea to use your real name.

Suddenly, over the LOUDSPEAKER:

> LOUDSPEAKER
> Telephone call for Mr. Truitt.

EXT. HOOVER HIGH SCHOOL – PARKING LOT – DAY (M.O.S.)

MUSIC UP. Bill is hurrying to his car.

EXT. BILL'S HOUSE – DAY (M.O.S.)

Bill drives up; Matt meets him at the car. Together they talk as they walk into the house.

INT. BILL'S HOUSE – DINETTE – DAY (M.O.S.)

Bill makes his way through the house to the dinette, where he sees Dedee alone in the backyard. Bill calls her name; she turns to us, tearful. CAMERA STAYS in the dinette as Bill leaves, goes outside, joins her in the backyard. As she hugs him, she looks around the backyard.

> DEDEE (V.O.)
> Can you believe this place? Gays love houses. I'd already worked on the beautiful dumb one. He helped out.

We see Matt explaining things to Bill; Bill resisting; Dedee chiming in eagerly . . .

> I laid it on kind of thick about Mom drinking and how tough it was on me watching my step-dad die, which was like so opposite, and how it would give Mom and me a chance to grieve in our own ways if there was a little distance between us.

Matt pleads with Bill. He's hard to resist.

> Just for the summer. Plus I'd clean for them, or tell their maid places she missed. Bill was like the definition of a softie.

INT. GUEST ROOM – NIGHT

Dedee is on the phone to her mother. Bill paces.

> DEDEE
> Okay. Okay, I promise. Okay. Bye, Mom. Yeah, here he is.

She hands the phone to Bill.

BILL
(*into phone*)
Hello? Hello, Bobette. I'm sorry about your loss. Yeah. Well, no one has it coming . . . Okay. Well, anyway . . . I can't hear you. No, it's just the ice against the glass, I guess. Uh-huh. Yeah, sure. I wasn't expecting – oh, he did? I don't know if he can get her a job, he's only the assistant manager . . . It's a Kinko's. Uh-huh. Okay, okay, we'll be in touch. Right. Bye-bye.

He hangs up. A beat.

Whoa.

DEDEE
She said I could stay till the end of the summer, right?

BILL
She's taking it hard. The death.

DEDEE
Taking it hard, yeah.

SUBLIMINAL CUT: BOBETTE AND SOME GUY

. . . rolling around on a bed.

BACK TO SCENE

BILL
Last time I saw you and your mom you were five. Dad's funeral.

DEDEE
I appreciate this, Bill. Really. I won't be in the way.

BILL
Hey. Family.

He kisses her, leaves. She goes to the door, peers out.

DEDEE'S POV – HALLWAY

Bill and Matt in the hallway, heads together. Matt's just showered; he's got a towel around his waist. Bill's arm is on Matt's shoulder. It's a good pair of shoulders, a good back.

> DEDEE (V.O.)
> Matt didn't look like a fairy at all. But it wasn't hard to see why he'd screw around with Bill. It was a great house. And a blow-job is a blow-job, if you're getting one. If you're giving one, it's harder, but even so . . . It's like Rule One about sex: if you don't breathe in, a person can do almost anything for ten minutes. Everything was going great until she showed up.

EXT. BILL'S HOUSE – DAY (M.O.S.)

Evening, but still light out. MUSIC. LUCIA (pronounced LOOSHA) DALURY pulls up in her car. She slams the door shut. Not even thirty-five, she already yells out her window when kids cut across her lawn. It's her sincere belief that happy people aren't paying attention. She heads into the house.

INT. BILL'S DINETTE/LIVING ROOM – DAY (M.O.S.)

In the background we can see Lucia arguing with Bill and Matt.

Meanwhile, Dedee, in the living room, examines the photos on the mantel, occasionally looking towards the kitchen and Lucia.

> DEDEE (V.O.)
> The sister of the dead guy. That's how Bill met him. She teaches next to him and one day she introduces him to her brother. This is like eight years ago.

We see older photos of Bill and Tom – Lucia's brother. Ten years ago. A younger Lucia. Moving into the house. Dog. Then a picture of Tom, much much thinner.

> She probably thought they could, you know, fish or play ball together, and they end up with their dicks in each other's mouth. She looked like she never got over it. Face like a cat's ass.

Dedee finds an urn on a shelf. She looks inside.

> Gross. But notice how pretty the jar is. That's typical gay.

EXT. YARD — TABLE AND CHAIRS — PATIO — DAY

Evening, but still light out on the deck of Bill's house. Dedee and Lucia are drinking coffee; Bill and Matt are in the dining room, clearing. Lucia is trying to like her. She's just been asked how to say her name.

LUCIA

Lucia. Lucia Dalury.

DEDEE

It's weird. How do you spell it?

LUCIA

L-U-C-I-A. It should be Lu-chee-a, but when I was a kid learning how to spell, I figured out they were saying it wrong. Because my sisters were named Marcia and Tricia. You know, C-I-A, 'SHAH'. So I figured my name should be pronounced Loosha. And it stuck. I kind of like it now.

DEDEE
(*as if Lucia couldn't be more pathetic*)
Yeah. Makes you different. Do you have a cigarette?

LUCIA

No.

DEDEE

Matt told me about your brother and Bill. Sorry he's dead. Did he give it to Bill?

LUCIA

What? I'm . . . that's none of your business.

DEDEE

Well it is, kind of. I mean, I might drink out of the same cup accidentally or something. If I stay for a while.

LUCIA

What do they teach you in Louisiana?

DEDEE
(*not insulted*)
It's roughly like, 'God works in mysterious ways.' If you get my drift.

LUCIA

You don't get it from cups. Anyway, they're both negative. Do you know what negative means?

DEDEE

Bill's kind of cute, isn't he? Even though he's old.

LUCIA
(*protesting*)

He's thirty-five.

DEDEE
(*not taking that as a contradiction*)

Yeah. But he's kind of cute. He looks like my father. I have a picture.

Dedee fishes in her wallet and drags out a color snapshot wrapped in Saran. She shows it to Lucia.

He married Bill's mom first. Then he fell in love with Miss Selectric. She typed 145 words a minute and went around the country demonstrating Selectrics in tight sweaters. There's a picture of her in the manual. When that broke up he married my mom. That's the one that killed him.

                              LUCIA
Yeah, you can see the resemblance.

Dedee watches Lucia watching Bill inside in the dining room.

                              DEDEE
Too bad he's a fairy, right?

Lucia looks at Dedee, alarmed at her perspicacity.

                              LUCIA
I wouldn't put it like that.

                              DEDEE
Well, then, too bad he's the way you'd put it.

She catches Matt's eye inside and smiles at him.

                          DEDEE (V.O.)
Matt worked the night shift at Kinko's most of the time, so he didn't go in until four. We hung out a lot.

EXT. BILL'S BACKYARD – POOL – DAY

Dedee sits at the end of the pool, her legs in the water, and eats cheeseburgers from a takeout bag as she watches Matt swim. He's got one of those bodies that respond to ten sit-ups and once in a while not having cake.

                          DEDEE (V.O.)
He was like a blind person, you know? They can't see but they hear real well. Matt couldn't think at all, but he looked great. It's survival. Cute stupid people survive and have lots of cute stupid babies who also survive. It was like watching evolution at work – as long as he reproduced.

Matt hoists himself out of the pool, sits next to her, grabs some fries from her bag.

                              MATT
So we figured, what the hell, and I moved in here. That was a year ago this June.

                              DEDEE
So it's like . . . if you were normal, you'd be in love?

MATT

We are normal. But I don't know. In love. He's like . . . I think he was in love with Tom.

DEDEE

You knew him?

MATT

No. Just from what his sister says. Bill doesn't talk about him.

DEDEE

He's like, what? Twenty years older than you?

MATT

Nine. Sometimes ten, depending on the month.

DEDEE

So. Have you always been a 'mo?

MATT

I guess, yeah.

DEDEE

You never slept with a girl?

MATT

Nope. It never came up.

DEDEE

So to speak, right? Good one.

Matt looks puzzled.

MATT

It's just not for me.

DEDEE

How do you know if you never tried it?

MATT

I never tried Communism but I know I wouldn't like that. It's the same thing. Or grits.

DEDEE

Have you ever had sex with a black person?

MATT

No.

DEDEE

Because you know you wouldn't like it.

MATT

I don't know that.

DEDEE

So even though you've never tried either, you'd have sex with a black person but not with me. God. That's like reverse discrimination. Quotas.

MATT

Is it?

DEDEE

Yeah. You're not giving white people a chance. You'd probably sleep with a Communist black person before a girl like me. It's prejudiced. Would you mind?

She's on her stomach. She hands him the lotion. He puts it on her back. The top of her swimming suit is undone. Suddenly, she rolls over on her back, exposing her breasts to him.

MATT

You can reach there yourself.

DEDEE

Scared you'll get a woody?

MATT

Look, Dedee, you're really nice, but I'm gay –

DEDEE
(*holding up her forefinger*)

Theory.

MATT

Whatever, and you're my boyfriend's sister.

DEDEE

Half-sister. Look, I get it, okay? If I were you, and I had this great set-up, and the guy I was with was like fifteen years older than me, and all I had to do was blow him a couple times a year, I wouldn't rock the boat either. You're a homo. Fine. Whatever. Like I give a shit.

She closes her eyes, lies back on the bricks. Matt's thinking.

MATT

Nine, ten at the most. Years older.

DEDEE

He could be your father. You are basically blowing your father. That can't feel right.

MATT

I never knew my father.

DEDEE

You really think this is a good way to make up for it?

She puts on some lip gloss with her eyes closed. Matt watches her, thinking . . .

INT. HOOVER HIGH SCHOOL — LIBRARY — DAY

A couple of weeks later. After school. End-of-school-year bulletins on the board. Bill's correcting papers. He doesn't look too happy. Lucia comes in, sees him, crosses to the window, pulls it open, lights a cigarette. On the sill outside are lots of butts.

LUCIA

You look like shit.

BILL

You have the window behind you.

LUCIA

Second of all, I don't trust her.

BILL

Who?

LUCIA

Dedee. Delta Dawn. God, Bill, don't you ever get tired of denial?

BILL

It kind of grows on you, as the years go by. Like disco.

LUCIA

You could send her back home. Not could, should. You're a teacher. She's a sixteen-year-old girl who should be in school somewhere. You're contributing to truancy.

BILL

We're out in three weeks.

LUCIA

She's running around town unsupervised . . . And she's a bad influence on Matt.

BILL

Matt's twenty-six.

LUCIA

Mentally? Emotionally? It's reverse dog years — you divide by seven.

BILL

Come on, Matt's a good guy.

LUCIA

He's not on your level. He doesn't know Japan's an island, for God's sake. He thinks the periodic table is something you teach in sex ed.

BILL

An archipelago. I think you can get through life without knowing Japan's an archipelago.

LUCIA

How you could go from Tom to him . . .

BILL

We're not going to have this discussion again.

LUCIA

No, what do I know about romance? I'm just the fag hag, right? I hate that.

BILL

Nobody uses that term anymore.

LUCIA

Tom used to.

BILL

We have a new word for women who prefer gay men to straight. It's 'women'.

LUCIA

What's the difference? Gay or straight, you all think with your dicks. I know it wasn't like that between you and Tom and so do you –

BILL

Listen, Lucia, Tom was great, Tom was terrific, that's who we were, Tom Terrific and Manfred the Wonder Dog, but he's dead. And you gotta move on.

LUCIA

You don't have to tell me he's dead.

BILL
And you don't have to tell me Matt's not Tom, okay?

Bill gathers his papers and leaves. Lucia yells after him.

LUCIA
You don't see what you don't want to see!
(*when he keeps going*)
Shit!

DEDEE (V.O.)
Could she be a bigger bitch? She called me the Swamp Thing once. You know what she needs, but who'd do it? So anyway, I'm there a month now, and things have developed . . .

INT. DEDEE'S BEDROOM — DAY

Late afternoon. Dedee and Matt are making love.

DEDEE (V.O.)
I know AIDS is like, awful and shit, and that guy who got all those boys up to his room and ate them and froze them and then he got killed in prison, like we cared, I mean, all that is disgusting. But they do look better than straight people. And smell better. They're cleaner, if you don't count viruses, and there's not all that hair in their ears and noses and shit. So it evens out. Anyway, Matt wasn't totally faggy. I mean, he knew what to do with it, believe me.

BEDROOM — LATER

It's dusk outside. Matt is staring up at the ceiling. Dedee looks at him.

DEDEE
I got bad news.

MATT
What?

DEDEE
I'm late.

MATT

Oh. Okay, I'll drive you.

DEDEE

No, I'm late. Like my period is late. Do you know what that means?
(*off Matt's look*)
I'm pregnant. We're pregnant.

MATT

You . . . you're kidding. We've been using condoms . . . Are you sure?
(*after a beat*)
Is it mine?

DEDEE

See? Only straight boys ever say that line. You're in, man.

MATT

No, I mean, don't get my hopes up if you're not sure.

Dedee looks at him. He wants the kid?

Seen from outside; we gradually approach the living room. We see an argument inside; hear voices . . .

DEDEE (V.O.)

We were going to break it to them in stages. One, we were in love. Two, surprise! We'd just gotten to stage one when Lucia dropped by. Typical.

INT. BILL'S LIVING ROOM – NIGHT

Bill, Lucia, Matt, Dedee. Bill looks like the world's caved in on him. That, and pissed.

LUCIA
(*to Dedee*)
I knew you were trouble. This is your brother here!
(*turning to Matt*)
And you! How could you?

MATT

It just happened. We didn't mean to hurt anyone.

LUCIA
You're gay, you jerk.

DEDEE
He just hadn't met the right woman.

LUCIA
Yeah, one with a dick.

DEDEE
Is that a cut?

MATT
For your information, I'm bisexual.

LUCIA
I went to a bar-mitzvah once, that doesn't make me Jewish! Please! Who says that bisexual shit besides gay men?

MATT
I'd understand if we couldn't go on living here.

LUCIA
You'd get that, huh? Congratulations.

MATT

It's just with the baby and all, it'd be easier.
> (*a beat as he takes in their expressions*)

Oh shit, that's not how we were gonna tell you.
> (*to Dedee*)

Sorry.

BILL

You're pregnant?

DEDEE

It was going to be a surprise.

Everyone looks at Bill. He sits down.

LUCIA

Do you want an abortion?

MATT

No! God. Look, Bill, if we could stay here till we get married and the baby comes . . .

DEDEE

Who said anything about getting married?

MATT

You don't want to get married?

DEDEE

You don't want to rush into something like that.

LUCIA

No, but bringing another human life onto the planet, that's Whim Time.
> (*to Bill*)

Am I the only one here who wants to kill someone?

DEDEE

You wish.

Bill stands up, looks at Matt. A moment, then:

BILL

I'll talk to you all tomorrow. I'm beat.

MATT

Bill –

LUCIA

Bill –

But he walks past them and up the stairs. Matt and Lucia look guilty. Dedee lights a cigarette.

LUCIA

Smoking's bad for the baby.

DEDEE

Like you give a shit. Or maybe somebody else mentioned abortion.

LUCIA
(*to Matt*)
You're breaking his heart.

MATT

I'm a little late for that.

He leaves, heads upstairs.

DEDEE

Where you going? Matt!

The two women are left alone. Lucia snaps her fingers at Dedee's pack of cigarettes. Dedee passes her one.

LUCIA

At least he knows what Matt's like now. You're probably a blessing in disguise. A fucking great disguise.

DEDEE

God. How does a woman end up so bitter?

LUCIA
(*taking a deep drag of her cigarette*)
Observation.

INT. MATT AND BILL'S BEDROOM – NIGHT

Bill's brushing his teeth in the door of the bathroom; his gums'll be bleeding if he doesn't calm down. In front of him in the bedroom Matt is packing a duffel bag.

> BILL
>
> She's under seventeen, you know. And she's my sister.

> MATT
>
> I didn't take advantage of her.

> BILL
>
> She had a death in the family. She came to us for help.

> MATT
>
> Dedee said you'd be jealous.

> BILL
>
> What?

> MATT
>
> I'm going to have a kid. I'm going to have a normal life. And that pisses you off. Misery loves company.

> BILL
>
> Normal life? Fuck you, Matt. Fuck you.

> MATT
>
> Look, Bill . . .

> BILL
>
> Don't talk. Pack. Pack yourself, pack her, and get the fuck out of here.

He slams the bathroom door shut on Matt. Matt takes a breath.

> DEDEE (V.O.)
>
> So we couldn't stay. So Bill wasn't a total loser. I didn't care. But if we had to get out, let's really get out. I mean, Indiana bit. Hoosier *this*, losers.

EXT. BILL'S HOUSE – DAY

Next afternoon. Bill pulls into the driveway after work.

INT. BILL'S HOUSE — KITCHEN — DAY

Bill enters from the garage. He's calmed down a lot.

                    BILL

Dedee?

INT. UPSTAIRS — DAY

Bill opens Dedee's guest-room door. It's empty. No suitcase, empty closets. He reaches for the phone. Dials a number. We hear a voice say, 'Kinko's.'

                    BILL

Could I speak to Matt? Matt Matteo?
           (*listening*)
Did he call in sick?

He listens, hangs up without saying anything.

INT. KITCHEN — DAY

Bill comes downstairs. There's a note on the refrigerator.

                DEDEE (V.O.)

I kinda felt sorry for him. I mean, he couldn't help being old. I said he was really nice, and thanks for the hospitality, and I apologized for taking the money, even though I didn't have to. Oh, and don't tell my Mom.

Bill puts the letter down and goes to the bulletin board. There's a ring of keys there. He flips through it. There's a key missing. He picks up the phone. Into it:

                  BILL

Yeah, business. First Guaranty Trust.

                DEDEE (V.O.)

Here's where he finds out we took the safe-deposit money. Ouch. Now he's covering for us, you know, not telling the bank it was unauthorized. Such a nice guy. Love him, hate me, right? People getting dumped are always lovable. Even homos. Wait, I can really lay it on.

The MUSIC gets STRINGIER. MONTAGE:

INT. BILL'S BEDROOM — NIGHT

Bill sits alone on his bed, puts his head on the pillow, rolls over to smell Matt on Matt's pillow.

INT. BILL'S HOUSE — UPSTAIRS HALLWAY — DAY

We DOLLY past pictures of Bill and Matt.

> DEDEE (V.O.)
> It's just tricks. It doesn't mean he's better than me. But you can't help yourselves. You see someone smell a pillow or an old sweater, you're a basket case. I coulda showed you the other stuff he did, besides mooning around. He ate like a pig, for one.

INT. KITCHEN — NIGHT

Bill eats alone.

INT. BILL'S HOUSE — HOME OFFICE/GUEST ROOM — NIGHT

Bill pays bills.

> DEDEE (V.O.)
> Like, he licked his plate, I'm not kidding you. He flossed, he clipped his toenails, he paid bills. Does that make your heart break? His boyfriend or whatever leaves and he pays the cable bill? So he wasn't like dying of pain. Even after she showed up.

EXT. BILL'S HOUSE — PATIO — NIGHT

Lucia and Bill, drinking coffee.

> LUCIA
> Did you call the bank? Are you sure?

> BILL
> Yeah. He signed the safe-deposit register Tuesday at noon.

LUCIA

How much was in it?

BILL

Ten thousand.

LUCIA

Thief.

BILL

Not technically. He was on the signature card.
(*picking up the portable phone*)
I gotta call her mother. She *is* a minor.

LUCIA

Wait a couple days. They'll call you – then you'll have something to tell her. You don't want the police involved. You're a schoolteacher. Come on.

He puts down the phone.

BILL

You're right. She's not my problem anymore. Neither is he. I don't have any problems. I'm fucking problem-free.

LUCIA

You are, Bill. You just don't realize it yet. You'll see.

EXT. BILL'S HOUSE – DAY

Morning. Bill's on his way to his car when someone calls his name. Bill turns, sees a guy in his early twenties: JASON BOCK. He looks ... well, radical. For South Bend. Pierced.

JASON

Mr. Truitt?

BILL

Yes?

JASON

What'd you do with Matt?

BILL

Excuse me?

JASON

Matt. Matt Matteo. Your boyfriend.
> (*off Bill's look*)

Mine too.

BILL

Who are you?

JASON

Jason Bock. I went to Hoover like four years ago. Look, don't pretend you didn't know about Matt and I. And don't worry, I don't do anything unsafe. I know what your lover died of.

BILL

'About Matt and me.'

JASON

I've been trying to call him for the last two days. No answer. He left his job. His car's not here. Where is he?

BILL

I have no idea. Now if you'll –

JASON

Hey, don't blow me off! I could make trouble for you. You know? Tell 'em you're gay –

BILL

They know I'm gay, you little prick.

JASON

– and you came on to me when I was a student. Do they know that?

BILL

That's a lie.

JASON

Tell me where he is.

Bill looks at him, deciding what to do. Jason is wincing, pulling his jeans away from his crotch.

New piercing.

BILL

Did he ever mention Dedee to you? My half-sister. She's visiting from Louisiana.

JASON

He's in Louisiana?

BILL

I don't know. But he took off with her. They're in love. That's what he told me. I don't know where he is.

JASON

He's bi? Are you serious?

BILL

We're always the last to know.

JASON

Fuck you. I want to talk to him. If I don't hear from him by Friday, I'm going to the police. For all I know you could have killed him.

BILL

Then for all you know I'm just getting started.

JASON

Get him to call me.

EXT. HOOVER HIGH SCHOOL — CLASSROOM — NIGHT

A classroom is lit up and we can see Lucia raging through the classroom windows. Bill's trying to calm her down. We CAN HEAR her muffled imprecations. She slams out of the room. He follows.

DEDEE (V.O.)

Lucia wasn't surprised that Matt had been screwing around. And that Jason prick had been in her homeroom for two years so she knew what he was like. After high school he went up to Chicago and became one of those ACT-UP people who think AIDS is like this big conspiracy against homos. Maybe it is, who knows. All I know is it isn't working. There seem to be more of them now than ever before, you know what I mean? They're tricky.

EXT. HIGH-SCHOOL PARKING LOT – NIGHT

Bill's following Lucia to her car.

BILL

Lucia, wait up!

LUCIA

Face it. He's gonna ruin you.

BILL

He just wants to scare me. He's angry. Matt dumped him too.

LUCIA

I don't know how you do it. So nice. So good. Tom was, too. It's depressing.

BILL

You're nice.

LUCIA

That's how I always felt around you two. Like the Baroness in *The Sound of Music*. Everyone's singing and climbing Alps and all I want to do is stuff that guitar up that nun's –

She stops as she sees a sheriff's car pull into the parking lot and stop beside their parked cars. Sheriff CARL TIPPETT gets out. He's a good tipper, but not so good it's insulting; and he gives the big candy bars on Halloween, never raisins.

CARL

Hey, Lucia, how are you? Hi, Bill. Got a minute?

BILL

Sure, Carl, what's up?
 (*to Lucia*)
See you tomorrow.

LUCIA

I can stay –

CARL

Actually, Lucia, it's business.

LUCIA

Actually, Carl, it's fine.

Carl looks at Bill, who nods.

CARL

Okay. Here's the deal . . . I got a stupid thing here I'm checking out. You know a Jason Bock?

BILL

Yup. Met him Tuesday.

CARL

Says when he was a student here four years ago, you molested him. I didn't like the look of him, but I gotta do something. I haven't told Walter yet.

BILL

But you'll have to, right? He's the principal. State law.
    (*pause*)
There's something else.

CARL

He filed a missing-person's report on Matt. Do you know where he is?

BILL

No, I don't.

CARL

This Jason creep mentioned something about a sister. I didn't know you had a sister. Half-sister.
    (*no response*)
Course if you say they moved somewhere, they wouldn't be missing. Even if we can't exactly find them.

BILL

They left me a note but I don't have it anymore. Where does that put us?

Carl sighs, moves to his car.

CARL

Shit, I don't know. Let me know soon as you hear from either of them.

BILL

You haven't asked me if it's true. If I molested him.

CARL

I'd like to send him someplace they will, for about five to ten. Might put some sense into him.

LUCIA

Only if his brain's in his ass.

CARL

Strikes me as fairly likely. Take care. We'll keep this under wraps as long as possible. Nice to see you again, Lucia. Long time.

LUCIA

Only a year, Carl. At the funeral, remember? Remember Nancy's funeral?

Carl looks puzzled. Bill intervenes.

BILL

Good night, Carl. We'll talk tomorrow.

Carl nods, gets in his car, drives off.

LUCIA

This is why I hate people. You always want to know why. Take it in.

BILL

Honey, I'm right there with you. Fuck that singing nun.

EXT. LUCIA'S HOUSE — DAY

Lucia walks down the sidewalk, picking up a newspaper as she heads to her Explorer. She puts it on the roof with her coffee cup as she opens the door. The newspaper blows off, lands face up NEAR US. We can read the headline: HOOVER HIGH SCHOOL TEACHER ACCUSED OF MOLESTATION. *In lower case, 'Admitted Homosexual 10-Year Veteran in System.' There's a picture of Bill, smiling.*

Lucia COMES TOWARDS US to pick up the paper. O.S. she reads it; then starts running to her car. She backs up quickly; the coffee cup, left on the roof, spins to the ground.

EXT. BILL'S HOUSE – DAY

Lucia pulls up, pushes her way through three or four reporters, some with video cameras. She knocks on the door.

LUCIA

Bill! It's me!
>(*to the reporters*)

You assholes –
>(*spotting one of them*)

Jennifer? Jennifer Oakes? Is that you?

JENNIFER, a TV reporter, photogenic and not much else, nods, a little embarrassed.

JENNIFER
(*as student*)

Hi, Ms. Dalury.
>(*as reporter*)

Any comment about the charges against William Truitt?

LUCIA
(*disgusted*)

I wrote you a letter of recommendation.

She uses her key, unlocks the door, slams it behind her.

INT. BILL'S HOUSE – FOYER, STAIRS – DAY

Bill's coming down the stairs, knotting a tie.

LUCIA

Jesus, Bill – did you know about this?

BILL

There were messages on my machine. I just heard them this morning. People'll believe anything.

LUCIA

Did you call that lawyer I told you about?

                         BILL
What for?

                         LUCIA
Hello? This is America. We don't like sodomy so much here.

                         BILL
Yeah, but the schools are good. Speaking of which –

                         LUCIA
You're not going in? Bill!

INT./EXT. BILL'S CAR/FRONT OF HIGH SCHOOL – DAY

A media madhouse. Lucia and Bill get out of the car and brace the crowd. Reporters thrust microphones at them; shout questions. Students watch in whispering, excited groups.

WE FIND a reporter checking her lipstick in the lens of a camera. She backs up, starts speaking:

                         REPORTER
Tanya and Clint, I'm here at Hoover High School where a sex scandal has exploded involving a high-school teacher whose seeming popularity may have been the cover for his predatory advances upon the young male students entrusted to him by this outraged and devastated community . . .

TV SCREEN – MONITOR – INTERVIEWS WITH STUDENTS

They're editing footage shot IN THE SCHOOL PARKING LOT back at the station:

                         BOY STUDENT #1
I had him for homeroom last year. I felt like, you know, he was undressing me with his eyes? And then he'd like leave me undressed for a good ten, fifteen minutes? Or sometimes he'd just put my socks back on?

                         GIRL STUDENT #1
Yeah, we know, we all know. I mean, hello? But he's not

really gay-gay, you know? Not like *Birdcage*. It's not like he like, you know, does makeovers on you and shit.

BOY STUDENT #2

I did notice at wrestling matches he was always watching the guys wrestle. But I mean, what else are you gonna watch? That's all there is, this circle with two guys wrestling in it. But maybe that's why he went, you know? Looking back . . .

GIRL STUDENT #2

This is America, we're all Christians here, aside from a few Jewish people, who are just born that way, and I can tell you one thing, Jesus Christ and his Apostles were certainly not into 'man-on-man' action, as they put it on their porno videos, which I'm proud to say Blockbuster does not carry. I work there and it's very family.
(*beat*)
Plus that religion John Travolta belongs to.

GAY MALE STUDENT

What gets me is this idea that a queer teacher does nothing but salivate all day. Because the straight boys are so desirable? Look around. These guys put the job in blow-job, you know what I mean?

INT. ADMINISTRATIVE OFFICES – OUTER OFFICE – DAY (M.O.S.)

The secretaries are bunched outside the principal's office, trying to eavesdrop on a meeting. They scurry away when the door opens and Bill appears. The PRINCIPAL appears behind him, looking unhappy at what he had to do. He shakes Bill's hand.

INT. BILL'S CLASSROOM – DAY (M.O.S.)

Students talking as a substitute writes her name on the board. Suddenly one of the students at the window says something; the rest of the students flock there.

THEIR POV – BILL

. . . walking to his car with boxes. Camera crews documenting it.

TV SCREEN – THAT FOOTAGE

... seen on the local TV show. A graphics banner across the bottom: SCHOOL FOR SCANDAL.

> DEDEE (V.O.)
> I'm just gonna give you the broad strokes here, because I've got my own problems with Matt which you'll find out about any minute. Bill got suspended with pay. It didn't even bother him. I guess when your first boyfriend – what's-his-name, Tom? – croaks in front of you and his stupid sister takes over your life, and then your next boyfriend splits, you're kind of primed for shit. It's hard to top that with suspensions and people hating you and losing a stupid job you're too rich for anyway. Lucia said it was denial, natch, what else? Bill just hired a lawyer, stayed at home, and worked on his garden.

INT. BILL'S LIVING ROOM – NIGHT

A rock sails through a window. Several other panes have been replaced with cardboard, and a broom and a dustpan stand ready. Bill, who's sitting in an easy chair, goes over to the rock, picks it up, hefts it in his hand, leaves the room ... CAMERA STAYS behind, lingering on the mantel. Some of us notice the dust ring where the urn with Tom's ashes used to sit.

EXT. BILL'S HOUSE – MORNING

The rock slips into place in the hillside rock garden. There's a lot of rocks.

> DEDEE (V.O.)
> Meanwhile, guess who was having the time of her life? Because her predictions came true. Between the time we left and that stupid phone call, which I can't go into right now, she was flying.

INT. BILL'S HOUSE – KITCHEN – NIGHT

Lucia, humming, cooks from a book.

INT. BILL'S HOUSE — DINETTE — NIGHT

Later, Lucia watches Bill eat.

>   DEDEE (V.O.)
> Look at the lipstick on her. She better hope it's drool-proof.

INT. BILL'S HOME OFFICE — NIGHT (M.O.S.)

Lucia is filing while Bill pays bills. She finds the manual to the Selectric typewriter. She opens it. There's a caption: 'Miss Selectric demonstrates her typing speed of 145 words per minute. It's easy on a Selectric!' But the face of Miss Selectric has been scratched out.

EXT. BILL'S LIVING ROOM — NIGHT (M.O.S.)

Lucia and Bill are watching TV. Bill tries to glance at the clock. Lucia is talking.

>   DEDEE (V.O.)
> You don't have to hear any of this – there's nothing going on here except her trying not to leave. Last night she went through a week of menus with him. Poor guy. Another night like this and he'll put her in the chair by the window.

INT. GROCERY STORE — DAY

>   DEDEE (V.O.)
> Look where she is. Men's Toiletries. The more private the better. You know what she's thinking? If only he had jock itch . . .

>   CARL (O.S.)
> Lucia?

Lucia, startled out of a reverie, turns to see Carl, the sheriff, smiling at her. The smile's not returned.

>   LUCIA
> Oh, hi, Carl.

She walks on with her cart.

>   CARL
> Hey, what a coincidence. Just talking to Bill. He sounds good.

LUCIA

No thanks to you.

CARL

It wasn't personal, Lucia, you know that.

LUCIA

Oh, I do, huh?

CARL

The kid's story's not going to hold up. The board'll clear him.

LUCIA

His reputation's ruined.

CARL

He never gave a shit about reputation.

LUCIA

Then he's got company. Nice seeing you –

CARL

Hey, hang on.
    (*he's trying to keep her there; he picks up a melon*)
I can't remember if Nancy said they should make a noise or not. What do you think?

LUCIA

Why don't you ask someone who gives a shit, Carl? Why don't you ask her nurse?

CARL

Sherry? She . . .
    (*realizing*)
Oh. So that's it. I didn't figure you for someone who'd listen to gossip.

LUCIA

Suppose you mind your business and I'll mind mine.

She moves off. Carl watches her, thinking.

EXT. BILL'S HOUSE – NIGHT

Lucia pulls in, her purchases beside her in the front seat. We notice the cardboarded window panes. We HEAR MUSIC drifting from the house. Uncharacteristic.

INT. BILL'S HOUSE – NIGHT

Lucia enters. There's loud MUSIC playing.

> LUCIA
> (*calling out*)
> I'm home! Bill?

Bill appears briefly at the top of the hall, empty suitcase in hand.

> BILL
> Hey!

Lucia's alarmed. She puts down the groceries.

> LUCIA
> What are you doing?

> BILL
> (*reappearing*)
> He called! He fucking called!

Lucia takes a moment, then climbs the staircase.

INT. BILL'S BEDROOM – NIGHT

Bill, energized, is throwing clothes into a suitcase. His phone is off the hook; the speaker button is lit. He is talking when Lucia enters.

> BILL
> Yes, from O'Hare to Los Angeles. Tomorrow. Early morning.

> OPERATOR
> We have flights at six, eight, eleven-thirty . . .

> BILL
> Eight. That's great. What time does that get into L.A.?

> OPERATOR
> Let's see. Nine-thirty, that's local time.

> LUCIA
> What the hell is going on?

OPERATOR

I beg your pardon.

LUCIA

Bill.

BILL
(to phone)

I'll call you back.
    (he hangs up)
Listen to this.

He presses play on his answering-machine.

ANGRY CITIZEN'S VOICE
(filtered)

Hey, is this the faggot? You fucking pervert –

BILL
(pushing a button)

Shit. No, here.

MATT'S VOICE
(filtered)

Hey, Bill? It's me. Are you there? Pick up. Shit. All right, I just wanted to call. I mean, it's been like months. Seems longer. Everything's cool. Maybe you're just listening to this. I can hang here for a while. Here's the number: 310-555-1063. You got that? So it's like seven-fifteen here, is it two hours different there? Anyway, just thought I'd say hi. Everything's cool. Dedee's getting real big. You should see her stomach. You can see these veins. Ugh. Anyway . . . Bye.

LUCIA
(after a moment)

Did you call back?

BILL

It's some kind of payphone.
    (he grabs a piece of paper from the night-stand)
L.A. Corner of Robertson and Santa Monica. I called Carl. He has this program with all the phone numbers in the U.S.

LUCIA

When?

BILL

I don't know. Maybe an hour ago.

LUCIA

I just saw him at the store.

BILL

Great, great, whatever. So look, can you keep an eye on the house when I'm gone?

LUCIA

You don't know where they're living.

BILL

I'll find them. I found the payphone.

LUCIA

But . . . why?

BILL
(*what he's telling himself*)
Are you kidding? To drag his sorry ass back here. To make him make that Jason kid take it all back. And to ship Dedee back to her miserable mother whether she likes it or not.

He continues packing, his spirits undiminished.

LUCIA

Just give that number to Jason. That's all he's interested in. He'll drop the charges then. And let her mother go out there and pick her up.

BILL

Hey, this is what I'm doing. I can get someone else to watch the house.

He disappears into the bathroom to pack some toiletries. Lucia thinks. Sighs. Picks up the phone, presses redial. Presses a '1', another '1', in response to a menu. Waits. Bill comes out.

Your problem is –

He stops as Lucia holds up a hand. Into phone:

LUCIA
Yeah. I need two tickets tomorrow, O'Hare to Los Angeles. Yeah. Morning. Dalury, Lucia. L-U-C-I-A. Hey, guess what, I know how my own name is pronounced. And Truitt, Bill. Sure.
(*to Bill*)
Hey, this is how it's gonna be. Don't piss me off.
(*into phone; annoyed*)
First? Yeah, right. It'll be Coach. You know how much this country pays teachers?

EXT. BILL'S STREET — DAY

A cab is waiting, Lucia's in the back seat. Bill is loading his luggage into the trunk. He gets inside, the cab pulls away. Behind them, and down the street, is a parked sheriff's car.

INT. CARL'S SHERIFF'S CAR (STATIONARY) — DAY

Carl watches the cab disappear; he starts his engine.

EXT. RENTAL CAR, CONVERTIBLE — (MOVING) — DAY

At first we just see a PARADE OF PALM TREETOPS as we pass underneath them. CAMERA TILTS DOWN to frame Bill and Lucia from behind as Bill drives.

BILL
Pretty, isn't it?

LUCIA
What's that smell?

BILL
Air.

LUCIA
It smells like a one-hour photo shop. But for blocks. How far is this hotel?

                    BILL

Coming up. Tom and I were here the year before he got sick, remember?

                    LUCIA
          (*looking up at the palm trees*)
I hear rats live up in them. Or is it bats? God, nature's sickening.

EXT. SANTA MONICA HOTEL — DAY

INT. SANTA MONICA HOTEL — HALLWAY — DAY

Lucia and Bill walk down the hallway. As they pass a Coke machine, Lucia sees a gay male couple bickering.

INT. LUCIA'S ROOM — DAY

Lucia closes the door behind her, looks at the room. There's a connecting door to Bill's suite. She unlocks it, then relocks it.

                    DEDEE (V.O.)
The thing is, I hate her guts, but there's more to her than meets the eye. Like there could be less. I'm not saying to know her is to love her. I'm saying to know her is to not want to kill her. Like, constantly.

Lucia tightens her lips, turns on the TV.

I know what you're thinking. She's like . . . so dead. But she had a life once. She just . . . I don't know. Stopped feeding it. So after a while it wandered away.

HOME MOVIES — SUPER 8 (1967)

Three girls, one of them fat, all under ten, dressing up a baby brother in a dress and high heels. The two girls are close to ten; the fat girl and the boy are more like five.

                    DEDEE (V.O.)
Marcia, Tricia, Lucia, Tom.

HOME MOVIES – SUPER 8 (1980)

Tricia's wedding. Lucia's a bridesmaid. Tom is an usher. Handsome.

> DEDEE (V.O.)
> She had a crush on him or something. Sick.

Eighteen-year-old Lucia watches Tom talking to another usher.

> This is just like in *The Godfather*. Watch.

INT/EXT. DALURY HOUSE (1980) – BACKYARD – DAY

Eighteen-year-old Lucia, still in her bridesmaid dress, checks on the buffet table.

She notices the soft drinks are running low. She goes through the house to the garage, a piece of cake in hand.

INT. DALURY HOUSE (1980) – GARAGE – DAY

Lucia enters, crosses to the garage refrigerator, starts loading sodas on a tray. Then she hears something which we don't. It's coming from the parked car behind her. The back door is open and the car is rocking. She goes towards it quietly. WHAT SHE SEES is her brother Tom, his pants around his ankles, on top of an usher. Then Tom looks around, sees Lucia. She's shocked. She drops the tray of soda bottles; they fizz at her feet.

> DEDEE (V.O.)
> You could tell it wrecked her; she was a virgin until she was twenty-eight. But she eventually sort of kind of maybe forgave her brother. She had to. No one else in the family could stand her. Besides, he was this broker in the eighties and he made a lot of money.

EXT. SOUTH BEND – LUCIA'S HOUSE – DAY (1990)

Lucia gets out of a car, stunned, in front of a house. There's a SOLD sticker and a big bow pasted on the FOR SALE sign. Tom and Bill are with her, smiling.

EXT. GRAND CANYON — CANYON TRAIL — DAY

A blonde woman on a burro rounds a corner. There's a burro there, riderless, looking over the canyon rim. The blonde woman calls a name, then kicks the burro.

> DEDEE (V.O.)
> Her dad died in the Grand Canyon. Something about a burro. His secretary lived. Lucia's mother died a year later. In a post office. She was mailing a book to Tom.

INT. MALL BOOKSTORE — DAY

A fifty-eight-year-old woman looks at a book, considering it favorably. We see the title: GOD MADE ME STRAIGHT: An Ex-Gay and Jesus Christ.

INT. SANTA MONICA HOTEL — LUCIA'S ROOM — DAY

Lucia is watching the TV.

> DEDEE (V.O.)
> Marcia lives in Saudi Arabia with her husband, who works for Texaco. She has cysts so no kids. And Tricia lives in Nashville. She's in retail. She has three boys who are big in Scouting.

TV SCREEN — 'THE SHOPPING NETWORK'

It's Tricia's Trinket Time. *Tricia is selling small wooden boxes for holding keys. She looks about how you'd expect.*

> DEDEE (V.O.)
> When Tom got sick, she visited once, then she got him on several prayer lists, whatever they are, which must've worked real well because he died like in a month. At Christmas she sends Lucia one of whatever item she couldn't sell to her audience. Lucia checks in during the year and makes bets on what it might be. It'll either be this or the quilted vacuum cleaner cover.

IN THE HOTEL ROOM

Lucia zaps Tricia with the remote. She starts getting ready for bed. She empties her makeup case onto the counter. She brushes her teeth without looking at herself in the mirror, which isn't easy.

> DEDEE (V.O.)
> None of this makes me like her more, but I thought you should know. Just to be fair. Meanwhile, I had my own problems.

EXT. HOLLYWOOD COURTYARD APARTMENTS – DAY

Pretty run-down, Wilcox-y.

> DEDEE'S VOICE
> Okay, okay. I got a t-shirt on and bikini pants. Are you serious? You're sick. Okay. Just a second.

INT. HOLLYWOOD APARTMENT – DAY

The inside matches the outside. Dedee's on the phone in the bedroom. We can really tell she's pregnant now.

> DEDEE
> *(faking it)*
> Okay, I took it off. Pretty tan, yeah. Uh-huh – I've got shoes on. High heels. You know my black ones I wore to the Holiday Inn?
> *(into phone)*
> Shit, I gotta go. Tomorrow? So what if it's Sunday? Whatever. Bye.

She hangs up, sighs.

INT. APARTMENT – LIVING ROOM – DAY

Dedee goes into the living room. Matt is standing there with a discarded crib. He doesn't look so hot. He's stooped. He needs a haircut. He's got a goatee. His skin is glistening unhealthily from sweat and chicken fat. He wears a Tacos Tacos uniform and has several cuts on his hands.

DEDEE

What is that?

MATT

Isn't it great? Trash day. You can't believe what people throw out.

DEDEE
(*unimpressed*)
Yeah, like garbage. Where's the food?
(*off his blank look*)
My nachos. You were gonna bring home a Nachos Supremo.

MATT

Shit, honey, I forgot. I'll go back.

DEDEE

How can you forget? Do you even think about me when you're there?

Matt approaches her. Takes her in his arms. It looks like a decision, not an impulse.

MATT

Course I think of you.

He tries to kiss her.

DEDEE

You smell like beans.

He keeps kissing her till she pushes him away.

Is that all you think about? Sex?

MATT

I don't know.

DEDEE

Because I'm sick of lying on my stomach.

She goes into the bedroom and slams the door. Opens it immediately to yell out:

Nachos, a Coke, and those little fried donut things with sugar, okay?

Matt nods, sits down, looks at the crib.

EXT. S. M. & ROBERTSON SHOPPING CENTER – DAY

The Pavillions in Boys Town. Lots of parking, lots of boys, a couple of strip mall shops. WE FIND Lucia by her car, surveying the area (and the male shoppers) with something less than enthusiasm. She turns to see Bill waving at a bank of payphones.

                BILL
              (*calling*)
It was this one!

                LUCIA
Great.

They meet halfway, squint at the shops in the center.

                BILL
I'll take half and you take half. The copy shop's a good bet.

                LUCIA
It doesn't mean he works here. He could do his shopping here.

But Bill's already flipping through some snapshots.

                BILL
You want to help or not? Up to you.

Lucia grabs some snapshots, heads off.

BOYS TOWN MONTAGE

Lucia and Bill with snapshots separately inquiring of cashiers, store managers, clerks: Have you seen this guy? The answer is always some version of 'No'.

INT. TACOS TACOS – DAY

Lucia and Bill carry trays to their seats.

                LUCIA
Maybe they're bad pictures. Maybe he's grown a beard or colored his hair or something . . .

                         BILL

Yeah. This was such a fucked-up idea. A guy makes a phone
call from a payphone in a city of 8 million, and I think I can
find him.

                         LUCIA

Look, Bill, if you're meant to find him, you will. Like you
ending up teaching at my school, and then me introducing
you to Tom. You know. Fate. It'll be the same with Matt. I
say we give this up and go home, and one day, if the gods
want you to see him again, he'll be sitting in the seat next to
you on a plane, or your cell-phone lines'll cross, or, I don't
know, his socks'll be in your dryer at some laundromat.
Destiny.

                         BILL

I don't believe in destiny.

                         LUCIA

Oh fuck, who does? It was worth a try.
                    (*she stands up*)
Excuse me. Bathroom.

INT. TACOS TACOS — RESTROOM AREA — DAY

*The women's door is locked. Lucia waits in this anteroom. There's a
door to the kitchen, a broken payphone, and a bulletin board. We SEE
it before Lucia: a picture of Matt as 'Employee of the Month'. She
almost misses it; she has her ear to the door, listening for signs of life
inside the bathroom. The door opens suddenly, she half stumbles into the
room, and the emerging FEMALE CUSTOMER gives her a look.*

*As Lucia enters the bathroom and turns to close the door, she sees it. It's
not what she wanted. She reaches up, takes it down.*

BACK AT THE TABLE

Lucia returns.

                         BILL

I was getting worried.

>   (*as he looks at her*)
> What? You okay?

A long moment as Lucia debates giving him the photo.

>   LUCIA
> The gods hate me. And if you ask me, they hate you too.

She takes the folded-up picture out of her purse, shows it to him.

> He works tonight.

EXT. TACOS TACOS – DAY (M.O.S.)

Just before sunset. Lucia sits on the hood of their car. Bill stands. The back door of the restaurant opens, and Matt emerges carrying two bags of trash. He heads for the dumpster. Bill calls his name. Matt turns, shocked. He freezes. Bill goes toward him. Lucia watches, sourly, as they talk, at first animatedly, then quietly. Matt looks over to Lucia. She forces a smile. Matt and Bill continue talking.

>   DEDEE (V.O.)
> Poor Bill. He shouldn't have come. Matt denied everything
> with that Jason guy, and Bill believed him. It must be inher-
> ited from our father, you know? Being romantic. It's just,
> when it's a man being romantic about a woman like Miss
> Selectric, it's not as revolting.

INT. BILL'S CAR – (MOVING) – NIGHT

Lucia's driving; Bill's riding shotgun. After a long moment:

>   LUCIA
> He looks like shit. That beard. And his posture . . . He looks
> like Early Man.

>   BILL
> He hurt his back lifting.

>   LUCIA
> I'm going to that dinner tomorrow. I got a few things to say
> to her. To him, too.

                    BILL
Hey, Lucia. I know what I'm doing.

                    LUCIA
You think so? You're like a lobster in a pot. All thrilled 'cause the water's getting toasty.

INT. BEVERLY HILTON HOTEL — ELEVATOR — NIGHT

The next night. First we see Dedee, trying to be composed.

                    DEDEE
Let me do the talking when we get to the money, okay?

Now we see Matt. He's shaved off his goatee.

                    MATT
Whatever.

INT. BEVERLY HILTON RESTAURANT — NIGHT

Lucia and Bill are already sitting at a table. They watch as Dedee and Matt make their way to them. Lucia notices how big Dedee is. Dedee's not surprised to see Lucia; just angry.

                    LUCIA
Jesus.

They get to the table. Bill stands. Lucia, her eyes on Dedee's belly, does a slow burn.

                    BILL
Hey.

                    DEDEE
                    (*to Bill*)
Hi.
                    (*to Lucia*)
Couldn't stay away, huh?

Matt pulls out a chair for her. She sits down, looks around.

                    BILL
                    (*to Matt*)
You shaved it off.

DEDEE
(*quickly, lying*)

I didn't like it.
(*an attempt at a smile*)
So. Are you enjoying your stay here?

BILL

I don't know if that's the word.

LUCIA

Can I ask you something, Dedee? When did you meet Matt? Refresh my memory.

A waiter, TIMOTHY, has arrived.

TIMOTHY

Good evening, folks, my name is Timothy and I'll be your waiter tonight. Beverage?

DEDEE

Yeah, I'll have a Long Island Iced Tea.

BILL

Is that a good idea? For the baby?

DEDEE

This baby owes its life to Long Island Iced Tea, if you know what I mean. Lots of ice.

LUCIA

Diet Coke.

BILL

Diet Coke.

MATT

Diet Coke. I mean, real Coke.

DEDEE
(*to Timothy*)

Do you have Bananas Foster on your dessert menu?

TIMOTHY

No.

DEDEE
Someone told me you had Bananas Foster.

TIMOTHY
I'm sorry.

He leaves. Dedee's pouting.

DEDEE
It's like impossible to get Bananas Foster.

MATT
Maybe they'll make it for you. If you describe it.

DEDEE
What about the sauce? You think they have the sauce just sitting around back there for Bananas Foster but they don't have Bananas Foster on the menu?

BILL
(*his schoolteacher voice*)
I appreciate you guys both agreeing to meet with me –

DEDEE
With you, not her.

BILL
– because there's a lot to talk about. A lot of reasons why you're coming back with us to Indiana.

DEDEE
I'm not going back.

BILL
You're sixteen. You're going to have a baby. Matt, you can't support her on what you make at that job.

DEDEE
That's for sure. Matt doesn't want to get legal, but you guys were kind of man and wife, so he should get half of what you have.

LUCIA
Are you serious?

BILL
That's not going to happen, Dedee. And if that's what you're thinking –

LUCIA
What about the $10,000 he stole?

DEDEE
He was entitled!

MATT
I'm really sorry about that, Bill –

BILL
You fucked up there. You're going to have to pay that back –

DEDEE
Hey, this isn't about *us* giving *you* money.

Throughout, Timothy torments them with ill-timed, over-solicitous service. In spite of him:

LUCIA
I'll tell you what it's about, Dedee. It's about timing. It's about trimesters. Do you know what I'm talking about?

DEDEE
(*she does*)
Like I'm going back to school? Come on, Matt –

LUCIA
You made a mistake coming here. You should have stayed home and sent Matt to do your dirty work. I've taught high-school girls for fifteen years, so pregnancy's one of my specialties. From the looks of you, you're five months pregnant, easy. Five-and-a-half, even. So that can't be Matt's baby.

A silence from everyone. Finally:

DEDEE
You're crazy. She's crazy. Let's go.

MATT
You're in your third month, right?

LUCIA
Yeah, when she met you.

DEDEE
Hey, I put on weight, big deal. What the hell do you know about it anyway? Like you've ever been pregnant!

MATT
She eats all the time.

LUCIA
It's not your baby, Matt. It's some other schmuck's with an eighth-grade education and a trunkful of Waco pamphlets. You don't owe her or that baby anything.

DEDEE
What the hell is your problem, lady –

BILL
Dedee? Is it Matt's?

Dedee's trapped. She's about to speak when –

MATT
Hey, it's her baby, isn't it? Whoever the father is. And I don't know how you figure I don't owe my wife's baby anything.

Another silence, equal to the first.

BILL
Your wife?

MATT
We got married in Vegas.

DEDEE
(*smiling*)
I can't wear the ring because I'm all swelled up, but it's nice. Color, clarity, carat. The three Cs of diamond buying.

BILL
But . . . who's the father? He's got rights and responsibilities . . .

DEDEE

My stepfather, if you want to know. And he's got the responsibility to rot in his grave which I hope he's living up to.
(*to Lucia*)
That make you feel better?

LUCIA

I don't believe you. You'd say anything. Maybe you should try saying it to the police –

Dedee reaches into her bag. She brings out the urn that used to be on Bill's mantel. Everyone, even Matt, is stunned.

Where did you get that?

Dedee opens it, turns it over onto the tablecloth. It's empty.

Where are the ashes?

DEDEE

Don't worry, they're zip-locked. If you want them back, stop following me, cover my expenses, and leave me alone. Matt?

She gets up and leaves. Matt looks quickly to Bill.

MATT

Shit, I didn't know.

He gets up quickly and follows. Lucia and Bill look at the empty urn.

LUCIA

Tom . . .

BILL

I'm going to kill her.

AT THE ELEVATOR

Dedee and Matt are getting in when Bill pulls her back. Lucia is right behind him. Timothy watches . . .

BILL

Hold on, Dedee!

MATT

Hey, don't grab her.

                    LUCIA
Shut up, Matt. I want my brother's ashes, you little bitch!

Dedee pulls herself free.

                    DEDEE
Hey! I didn't want to take them. I did it for insurance –

Lucia reaches out, tries to grab her.

                    LUCIA
You are one heartless little –

                    DEDEE
Yeah, no heart, Lucia, that's me. What body part are *you* missing?

The elevator doors close and they go down. Lucia is near tears. Bill is deeply, coldly angry. We've never seen him like this. He looks up at the elevator.

                    BILL
Shit.

Discreetly, Timothy points to a door marked STAIRS.

INT. BEVERLY HILTON STAIRWELL – NIGHT

Bill and Lucia are running down the stairs.

EXT. BEVERLY HILTON – NIGHT

Dedee and Matt's car pulls out of the hotel parking lot into the street. Bill and Lucia run to their rental and follow them.

EXT. HOLLYWOOD STREETS – NIGHT

Bill and Lucia follow Dedee and Matt. These are very unglamorous Hollywood streets.

                    DEDEE (V.O.)
They're just ashes, you know what I'm saying? Who knows if they're really his anyway? You really think they keep them separate? Please. And don't get all righteous and try to impress yourself by hating me. Go ahead if you want to but

look at them. They've never had more fun in their lives. These are teachers, remember. It's this or clapping erasers in South Bend.

EXT. WILCOX AVENUE — NIGHT

Bill's car pulls over.

INT. BILL'S CAR — (STATIONARY) — NIGHT

Bill and Lucia watching . . .

THEIR POV — DEDEE AND MATT

. . getting out of their parked car, crossing the street into a rundown courtyard apartment.

BACK TO BILL AND LUCIA

          LUCIA
Now what?

          BILL
Do you want the ashes back?

          LUCIA
I wanted you to divvy them up, remember? Just in case something like this happened.

          BILL
Yeah, I don't know why I didn't see this coming.

          LUCIA
You don't have to be sarcastic.

          BILL
I say we wait. He'll go to work in the morning, she'll go out looking for Bananas Foster, whatever the fuck they are, and we break in and find them.

          LUCIA
Great. Our first felony.

                                BILL
        I'll get you a cab back to the hotel.

She glares at him, pulls her sweater around her, settles down for the night . . .

EXT. WILCOX AVENUE — DAY

Morning.

INT. BILL'S CAR — (STATIONARY) — DAY

Bill and Lucia are asleep; Lucia's nestled against his side.

EXT. MATT AND DEDEE'S APARTMENT — DAY

Matt leaves the apartment building, crosses the street to the car. Starts it, pulls out.

INT./EXT. BILL'S CAR — (STATIONARY) — DAY

Later. Bill wakes up, notices that Lucia's nestled next to him, her face nuzzling his chest.

He gingerly tries to extricate himself. She wakes up, realizes slowly where her face is. Mortified, she tries to recover her composure.

                                LUCIA
        Oh. Sorry. I . . .

                                BILL
        No, no, it's fine.

                                LUCIA
        Oh my God, is that — did I drool?

                                BILL
        It'll dry, forget about it.

                                LUCIA
        Usually I have to be up a few hours before I'm humiliated.

                                BILL
                (*looking at the apartment building across the street*)
        You and me both. Come on. Let's get out of here.

                              LUCIA
>   Wait – look!

A TEENAGER

... pulls up in a real beater with Louisiana plates. We recognize him as Randy, Dedee's duped Christian boyfriend from Crevecoeur. CAMERA TURNS to find Dedee in the courtyard of her apartment. Randy approaches her. They kiss. She leads him back into the complex.

BACK TO BILL AND LUCIA

They are shocked. Crouching down in their seats:

                              LUCIA
>   My God. She's the Human Tabloid.

                              BILL
>   Where's Matt? You see his car?

EXT. TACOS TACOS – PARKING LOT – DAY

Matt's car pulls in, goes around to the back. His hat and apron are on the seat next to him. He stares ahead at the dumpster, where he met up with Bill two nights ago.

Suddenly he backs up, swings past the dumpster, and pulls out of the parking lot. We stay on the dumpster: his hat and apron are now resting on top of it ...

EXT. SIDE OF THE APARTMENT BUILDING – DAY

Bill is quietly picking his way down the side of the apartment building. A line of bamboo hides him from the neighbors. We HEAR a lot of daytime TV coming through the windows he passes. Lucia's right behind him.

                              LUCIA
                           (whispering)
>   What are we doing?

He turns to her, waves her to stay put – but she doesn't.

>   Come on, let's go back to the car.

                          BILL
    I want to find out what the fuck is going on here.

They reach the last window. The RADIO is ON here, LOUD.

    I can't hear a thing.

                          LUCIA
    Good. Let's go.

                          BILL
    Just a second.

He raises his head, peers inside.

BILL'S POV — DEDEE AND MATT'S BEDROOM

Randy's on his back, his pants down around his ankles. Dedee's on top of him, clothed, moving up and down.

BACK TO BILL

. . . as he ducks down.

                          LUCIA
    What?

                          BILL
    I think we found the father. Of the next one, anyway.

Lucia peeks.

LUCIA'S POV

Behind the rising-and-falling Dedee, the TV, on MUTE, shows the Shopping Network — and Lucia's muted sister.

BACK TO LUCIA

She tears herself away, sinks down next to Bill.

                          LUCIA
    That can't be good for the baby.

                          BILL
    Not only this, she'll smoke a cigarette after.

Behind them, in the apartment, we HEAR Dedee CLIMAXING. Then Randy.

> LUCIA
> I hate to say it, but poor Matt.

> BILL
> (*starting to leave*)
> He made his bed, he can lie in it. If there's room. Come on!

But suddenly Dedee's right above them, trying to yank the window open wider. The screen falls off and lands on Lucia, who freezes.

> DEDEE
> Fucking window. God, I'm sick of this city.

Bill stops, crawls back. Dedee lights a cigarette, throws the match outside, and turns back into the room. Bill and Lucia breathe again.

> DEDEE (O.S.)
> It's not gonna do any good. I've looked everywhere.

> RANDY (O.S.)
> You're sure he didn't lose it like he said?

> DEDEE (O.S.)
> I was watching him the whole time he was in the casino. Besides, he's too wimpy to gamble.

Lucia mouths to Bill: 'Your money.'

Randy, forget about it! I'm hungry. Let's go.

WE HEAR a DOOR OPENING.

> RANDY (O.S.)
> What's that?

> DEDEE (O.S.)
> Shit.

> MATT (O.S.)
> Honey? I told you to keep the door locked.

Bill and Lucia see a leg suddenly thrust itself out the window – and then stop suddenly.

195

Hey! What the fuck –

Randy is at the window, trying to get it open. He gives up, turns around. As he does we go:

INT. DEDEE AND MATT'S BEDROOM, HOLLYWOOD – DAY

Matt is standing at the door, seeing Randy in his underwear.

DEDEE
You're supposed to be at work till three.

MATT
I quit. We're going back home. Who is he?

Stupidly, Randy tries affability.

RANDY
Hey, Randy Cates, man. How ya doing?

MATT
Fuck you.

Randy starts dressing as Dedee handles Matt.

DEDEE
Matt, he's a friend from home. He wanted to use the shower. You know how it is after a long drive.
(*to Randy*)
Why don't you get in the shower now?

MATT
Why don't you get the fuck out of here?

RANDY
Hey, man. Be cool. I come in fellowship.

MATT
I said get out of here!
(*to Dedee*)
You think I'm stupid?

DEDEE
What do you mean, we're going home?

MATT

This isn't how it's gonna be. You don't go around stealing people's ashes, you know. It was bad enough taking the money –

DEDEE

You took the money –

MATT

Well, I'm giving it back.
> (*he realizes he's made a mistake*)

I mean, what's left of it.

DEDEE
> (*to Randy*)

See? He lied to me.
> (*to Matt*)

You didn't lose it in Vegas. Where is it?

MATT

You're not getting it. It's for the baby. I meant what I said. I don't care who the father is, I'm going to raise it, and so are you.

DEDEE

That's my money!

RANDY

What do you mean, it's not your kid? It's not his kid?

DEDEE

Whose do you think it is, Randy? Mr. Who-Needs-A-Rubber-I'll-Pull-Out-In-Time?

MATT

You said it was your stepfather's –

DEDEE

Come on, Randy!

Matt looks from her to Randy.

MATT

Is this the guy with one ball?

RANDY

Hey! Dedee!

DEDEE

We're out of here, Matt. It's his baby and we're going to start fresh, right, Randy? It's God's will.

Randy rises to the challenge.

RANDY

Yeah, I guess so. I wish his will had been for me to wear a rubber, but . . .
        (*he shakes himself together, turns to Matt*)
. . . that's life, so . . . we need the money. See what I mean? For the baby.

MATT

No way.

DEDEE

Come on, Matt. Come on.

She sidles up to him; suggestively:

> It's not gonna work out between us. You're gay. I don't mind so much, but I want my kid to have a real father.

MATT

I told you I was gay!

RANDY

This guy's a homo?

MATT

Could you just leave us alone now?

RANDY

What about AIDS?

DEDEE

That's where the ashes come in, but don't worry about it.

RANDY

You haven't been doing it with him, have you? He's probably getting it all over the baby!

He turns to Matt, starts pushing him.

That's an innocent child in there, you sonofabitch.

DEDEE
Hey. Randy! Be Christ-like!

MATT
Don't do that, man.

RANDY
Fucking faggot!

Matt hauls off and punches Randy. It's a good punch; Randy hits the wall. But it's made him furious. He lunges at Matt. They punch each other, rolling around the floor.

DEDEE
Hey! Hey!

Suddenly there's a gunshot. Dedee's holding the gun. The bullet buries itself in the mattress. Matt and Randy stop fighting.

OUTSIDE THE APARTMENT

Lucia and Bill hear the shot. Bill starts to get up but Lucia restrains him.

INSIDE THE APARTMENT

Matt and Randy, both bloodied from their fight, eyes round, wait for instructions. Dedee doesn't lower the gun.

DEDEE
Where's the money?

Matt looks up.

SECONDS LATER

The money is taped to the ceiling-side of a blade in the ceiling fan. Matt reaches up, removes it.

BACK TO SCENE

Matt hands the money to Dedee.

                    MATT
You're going to need money for the baby.

                    RANDY
We'll deal. Come on, Dedee.

                    MATT
Hey! The ashes!

                    DEDEE
I'll mail them to you if you're cool.

He sinks down on the bed.

                    MATT
When?

Dedee and Randy leave.

                    RANDY (O.S.)
What's all this shit about ashes?

EXT. SIDE OF THE APARTMENT BUILDING — DAY

Lucia's at the front corner of the building, hiding behind a yucca, watching them hurry to Randy's car. She's aware of the gun, but she manages to get a few letters off the license plate.

                    LUCIA
T-C-8 something something something. Louisiana. T-C-8 —

She's expecting to see Bill right behind her. He's not. She looks back down the side of the apartment building.

LUCIA'S POV — BILL

. . . shoving Matt against the wall, not too roughly. Matt is refusing to fight back. Finally, Bill stops shoving him. Frustrated, he grabs hold of the fence, rattles it. Matt tries to calm him.

BACK TO LUCIA

She watches, resigned.

INT. SANTA MONICA HOTEL – BILL'S ROOM – DAY

Bill is packing his suitcase. The connecting door to Lucia's suite is open. She's glaring in that doorway.

LUCIA
Well, I think you're a fool, Bill, but it's none of my business –

The door to the bathroom opens and Matt comes out of the shower.

MATT
Wow, that's a really good shower.

LUCIA
Yeah. Sit down, Matt.

MATT
You see the sewing kit they give you?

BILL
Matt . . . I know you're sorry for what's happened.

MATT
You mean for stealing the money?

LUCIA
And my brother's ashes, and the trouble your boyfriend got Bill into at school –

MATT
He's not my boyfriend – I can't believe he said that –

BILL
Let's not go into any post-mortems, okay? Let's just go back home, see if we can straighten Jason out, and take it from there.

LUCIA
I'm sure Jason'll put you up, boyfriend or not. Because Bill doesn't want you back.

MATT
What about the ashes?

BILL
They're not Tom, okay? I'd rather they weren't bouncing around in some knapsack right now –

LUCIA

You wish. She's probably trying to smoke them.

BILL
(*as privately as he can to Matt*)
What I'm saying is, so things didn't work out between us, so it didn't last for ever, fine. Let's go our separate ways without a lot of bad feeling and bullshit.

MATT

Wow. I'm really surprised.

Lucia's in high spirits: they're going home.

LUCIA
(*breezily*)
This is how we do things on the planet Maturia. We have much to teach you here.

BILL
(*eyes on Matt; something's coming*)
Lucia –

MATT

Really surprised. I expected better from you. Well, maybe not from Lucia, but you, Bill. Come on. She's your sister –

LUCIA

What?

MATT

– pregnant, probably abused, with all sorts of repressed memories that haven't even occurred to her yet, she comes to you for help and instead you just let her go away with this violent stalker guy who tracked her down!

BILL

Now wait a minute –

MATT

She's in danger! You promised her mother you'd look after her, and now this guy who's pissed off at the world because of a physical abnormality which he will probably take out on Dedee . . .

LUCIA

I think she's pretty used to him taking out his physical abnormality. Taking it out and waving it around.

She looks at Bill, inviting him to laugh – but Matt's arguments are registering with him. Her smile fades.

BILL

I know she's technically a minor, but . . .

MATT

Come on, Bill. She's a kid. She's got no one to turn to, not her mother, her father is dead, her stepfather is dead, I lied to her about the money, and even her blood brother who she came to for help by bus, even he's washing his hands of her . . .

BILL

I should let her mother know?

Suddenly, Lucia explodes. She hurls herself at Matt –

LUCIA

I'm going to fucking kill you!

Bill grabs her, pulls her off Matt.

MATT

You're frustrated, Lucia, I understand that, I even share your feelings –

LUCIA

Prove it! Help me kill yourself!

MATT

But I also feel some responsibility to Dedee.
(*the truth now*)
And that baby.

Bill holds Lucia as Matt goes to the phone.

BILL

What are you doing?

MATT
(*into phone*)
Hi, yeah. I think it's a business. The police. Missing persons.

LUCIA
Let go of me!

Bill pushes her aside onto the bed. He takes the phone, slams it down.

BILL
Enough! Matt, sit down. Don't touch that phone! Lucia, take five. Go on. Get out. Go. I'll handle this.

LUCIA
(*in an undertone*)
Bill, come on. I don't think he's as dumb as we think.

BILL
As *you* think, Lucia.

LUCIA
God damn it! God damn both of you! I hope Tom Cruise is as straight as they come! I never thought he wasn't!

She slams out. We STAY ON Bill and Matt . . .

INT. SANTA MONICA HOTEL — GROUND-FLOOR HALLWAY — DAY

The elevator doors open and Lucia sees Carl standing there, surprised, guilty.

CARL
Hey. Lucia.

Lucia looks at him, dumbfounded, then heads outside.

EXT. SANTA MONICA STREET — DAY

Lucia walks, Carl chases after her. She raises her hand as if to flag a cab.

CARL
Lucia! Lucia! It's L.A. They don't have cabs.

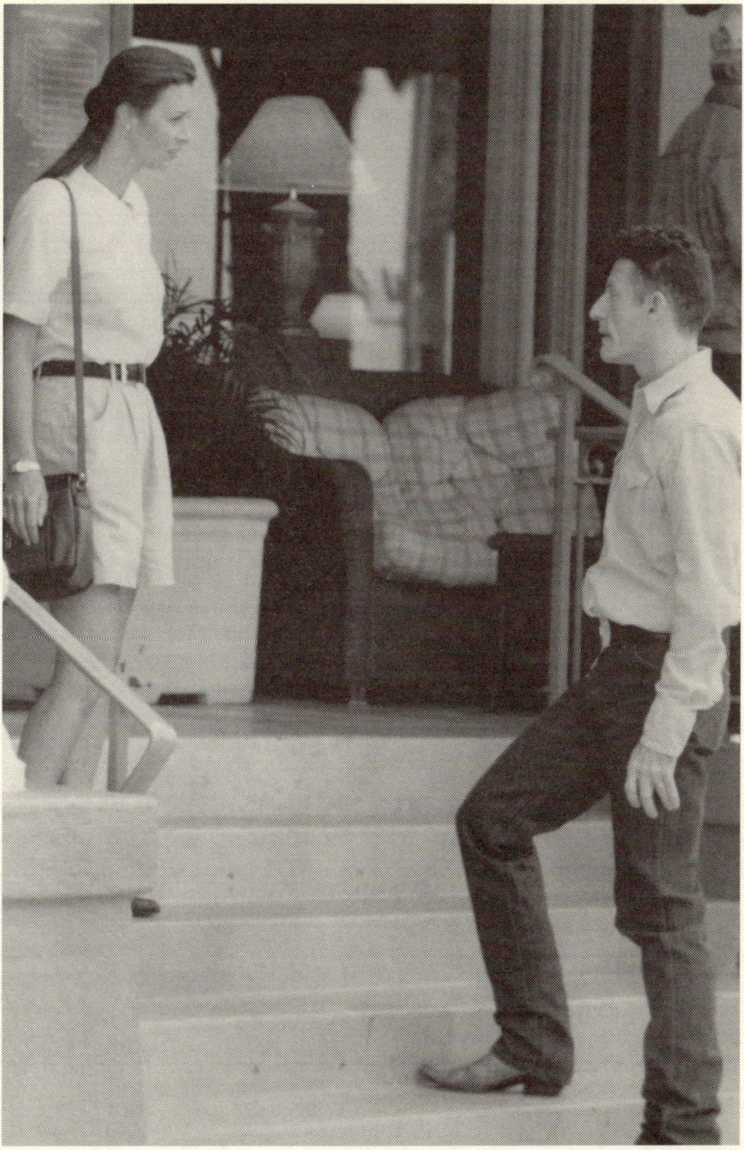

LUCIA

Leave me alone!
> (*to a passing car*)

Can you take me to the airport!

Carl reaches her, takes her arm.

CARL

Hey.

LUCIA

You want to arrest somebody? They're upstairs in 315. I'll testify. I'll be on the fucking jury.

CARL

I don't have any jurisdiction here. I'm here as a friend. Known him, what, twenty years. Longer than you.

LUCIA

Loyal to a fault, that's you.

CARL

Hey, Lucia. He's in trouble. The little shit who filed charges isn't withdrawing them. The school board is all politics – he might really lose his job. All he needs is this problem with the girl spinning out of control. I'm here to keep an eye on him. I get vacations like everybody else.

LUCIA

Really? Well, while you've been keeping an eye on him, there's been a gunfight, some grand larceny, a little extortion, and the transportation of a minor across state lines. When does the busting-down-the-door-and-saving-us-from-ourselves part come in? Right before we hijack Air Force One?

CARL

When was all this? Today? I was . . . visiting a friend.

LUCIA

Oh, yeah, she moved out here. What's her name? Terry? Cherry?

CARL

Sherry. What's your beef with me?

                    LUCIA

Nothing. Your wife was dying and you screwed her nurse. No big deal.

                    CARL

I was lonely.

                    LUCIA

That's all you've got to say for yourself?

                    CARL

If Nancy didn't mind, why should you?

                    LUCIA

Nancy knew?

                    CARL

What gunfight?

                    LUCIA

Like I'm talking to you? Like I would stoop that low?

                    CARL

Fine. You take the moral high ground. I'll be down here, looking up your dress.

He heads off. As Lucia watches him go, she has an idea.

                    LUCIA

Hey, Carl!
          (*when he turns back*)
Do you have any police buddies out here?

INT. SANTA MONICA HOTEL – HALLWAY – DAY (M.O.S.)

Lucia, talking non-stop, walks with Carl to Bill's room.

                    DEDEE (V.O.)

She's smarter than she looks. She knows Bill's going to do what Matt wants – find me. But if the police get involved officially, it'll be a scandal and Bill will never get his job back, and then who will she drool over in the faculty lounge?

INT. BILL'S MOTEL ROOM – DAY (M.O.S.)

Lucia, Matt, Bill, all talking at once. Carl paces in front of them, phone in hand.

CARL

Carl talks on the telephone.

DEDEE (V.O.)
So she gets Carl to call a local buddy, run Randy's license plate, and put out an unofficial APB on us. You gotta hand it to her. She always gets her way. And it's not sex appeal. Come on, she looks like a cafeteria lady. If they made a Lucia doll it'd come with a hair net, plastic gloves and her own working steam tray. She's beyond sex. Like amoebas.

INT. SANTA MONICA HOTEL ROOMS – NIGHT (M.O.S.)

Bill is pacing from Lucia's room to his. Matt's asleep in his bed; Lucia's dozing on hers.

CARL

Carl's watching Lucia. Suddenly, the phone rings. He snaps it up.

DEDEE (V.O.)
Anyway, some cop somewhere spots Randy's car.

EXT. PALM SPRINGS – DAY

Dawn. A policeman on the radio, looking off-screen. He listens, pulls out.

DEDEE (V.O.)
Which at least is gonna liven things up as far as I'm concerned. Because frankly, I'm starting to think Randy's missing more than a ball.

CAMERA SWIVELS to show us what the cop was looking at: a Palm Springs motel with Randy's car in front.

DISSOLVE TO:

EXT. PALM SPRINGS — MOTEL — DAY

Later. Randy's car is gone. In the back parking lot, we see a motorcycle, a bucket of suds, a hose.

INT. PALM SPRINGS MOTEL — DAY

Dedee's on the phone. The magic fingers on the bed are on; the mattress is vibrating.

> DEDEE
> (*into phone*)
> Right, what time is that? Okay, whatever. It's paid for, isn't it? Okay — oops, gotta go.

The door opens and Randy comes in, pissed.

> RANDY
> There's a big old rust spot on the chrome near the — were you on the phone?

> DEDEE
> My mom. She says hi.
> (*the Magic Fingers stop and Dedee slaps the metal box*)
> Did you talk to them about this piece of shit?

> RANDY
> I told you no phone calls.

> DEDEE
> You serious? You told me?

> RANDY
> Hey, come on. In a Christian family, the man is the guy, you know? It can't be like voting. I'm the guy, you're the wife and the mother and so on.

> DEDEE
> Yeah? This whole religion starts because some Jewish girl gets knocked up by someone who's not her fiancé, so she goes to the fiancé and says, Honey, I'm pregnant, I think it was the Holy Ghost or this bird, and incidentally I'm still a virgin, and from now on that's part of my name, and all the fiancé says is, Oh, okay, sure, baby: when's the wedding?

And you think the moral of this story is the man rules the roost?

RANDY

Phone calls in motels are rip-offs. We can't afford it.

DEDEE

We can't afford it because you spent $4,000 on that fucking bike yesterday.

RANDY

Can you watch your language please?

DEDEE

No, you watch my language, I'll watch my money. I want the rest of it right now. You can't handle it.

RANDY

It's the husband's job to decide –

DEDEE

Hey, Bible Boy, you're not my fucking husband. Now give me the fucking money.

RANDY

This is what happens when you talk to your mom. She gets you worked up.

DEDEE

She wants me to come home.

RANDY

We're not going back there.

DEDEE

There'll be a ticket at the airport by five.

Dedee goes into the bathroom. Randy is left alone in the bedroom. He's panicky. He goes to the door, bangs on it.

RANDY

Dedee, you can't go home! You need to stay here with me! I've prayed on this!

DEDEE (O.S.)
Pray on this, Parable Head!

Randy, desperate, goes to the night-stand, takes out Dedee's gun. He brings it back to the door.

RANDY
I've got your gun here!

A pause, then Dedee opens the door. She's unimpressed.

DEDEE
Oh, for God's sake. What are you going to do? Shoot me? Shoot yourself?

She takes it from him and throws it on the bed, which starts vibrating.

RANDY
Goddammit, Dedee, you don't treat me fair, you know? It's a lot of driving from Crevecoeur to here. You said come and I came, no stopovers or anything. And all I ask is that you stand by your man, you know, like I'm standing by you. Lot of guys woulda said, Hey, she took up with homosexuals. She's turned her back on righteousness.

DEDEE
But blowing you in the back seat of your car every day after band was a stairway to heaven, right?

Dedee drags her suitcase on the bed, starts packing, taking everything that isn't nailed down in the room. All the while she looks out the window.

RANDY
You waiting for somebody?

DEDEE
The guy from the bike shop. He's coming to take it back. The bike.

RANDY
(*dumbfounded*)
No, he's not.

She waves the pink slip and the sales contract at him.

DEDEE
That was my money, not yours. When I told the guy you bought it with stolen money, he decided he ought to take it back.

WE FOLLOW HER as she starts emptying the dresser drawers.

I'll leave you enough for gas to get wherever you're going, but I need the rest of it for when I get back to Louisiana. I don't intend to –

We're CLOSE ON HER when her face is slammed into one of the drawers, dazing her. WIDEN to show that Randy is standing over her, eyes unfocused, breathing hard.

RANDY
Why are you acting this way?

Dedee is on the floor, shaken. She shakes her head; tears are forming.

DEDEE
I think you hurt the baby.

Randy, back to his senses, kneels down to comfort her – and she kicks him in the groin. He reels back, clutching himself, swears. She goes for the door, but he grabs her, throws her backwards on the bed. We can't see much of what's going on.

We HEAR SOMEONE getting punched, and then we hear a GUN-SHOT, muffled by the blankets. Then total silence, aside from the SOUND OF THE MAGIC FINGERS. Now the CAMERA moves slowly over to the bed. Both bodies are vibrating slightly – but it looks like Randy's arm is moving while Dedee's legs are not. Then we realize Dedee, underneath Randy, has been moving his lifeless arm to get it off her. She sits up in bed. The back of his head is bloody.

DEDEE (V.O.)
What'd you think, I'd be the dead one? I'm the fucking narrator, guys. Keep up.

Dedee reaches over to Randy, feels for a pulse. He's dead. Definitely. She's horrified.

It'd be a lot easier for all of us right now if Randy was

someone we hated, but he was nice, mostly. Even I liked him. So in order to get you to swallow it, and not totally hate me, I'm gonna show you something that happens like in five hours.

INT. PALM SPRINGS CORONER'S OFFICE — NIGHT

The Medical Examiner speaks to the police officer. Randy's body is visible behind them.

MEDICAL EXAMINER
He had a very enlarged heart. He would have lived, I don't know. Not more than six months. Least this way he died quick. Never knew what hit him.

POLICE OFFICER
Yeah. Looks peaceful. Probably an orphan. But it's still murder.

MEDICAL EXAMINER
Just not as unlikable.

POLICE OFFICER
(*looking at the body*)
What is that, only one ball?

INT. PALM SPRINGS MOTEL — DAY

Right where we left off: Dedee is horrified, panicky. The sheets are covered with blood.

She stands up — and faints, falls back on the vibrating bed. It continues for a few seconds, then stops with a shudder.

CAMERA DRIFTS OVER TO THE PATIO WINDOW and the view of the mountains outside . . .

MATCH CUT TO:

THE SAME VIEW

Two hours later. CAMERA MOVES from the view past the bed and to the door. THERE'S A KNOCK.

EXT. SECOND-STORY BREEZEWAY — DAY

Matt is knocking on the door, frustrated. He leans over the railing, calls down:

MATT

No answer!

EXT. PALM SPRINGS MOTEL — DAY

Bill, Lucia, and Carl leaning against their rental cars in the nearly empty parking lot.

LUCIA

They're not here. This is ridiculous.
(*calling up*)
Come on, Matt, let's go!

CARL

Maybe they're down at the pool. Don't see the car, though.

BILL

Let's give him a minute.

LUCIA

If she's here, I want to talk to her.

BILL

That'll do a lot of good. She doesn't like you, Lucia.

LUCIA

A lot of people don't like me, doesn't mean I can't talk to them. Isn't that right, Carl?

CARL

That a lot of people don't like you? I'm gonna check the back for their car.

He heads off. Lucia's left with Bill.

LUCIA

I'll give him one more minute and then I'm sorry. We have to go.

                        BILL

Lucia, in eight years I don't think I've ever told you to shut up. Let's try for nine.

EXT. MOTEL – SECOND-STORY BREEZEWAY – DAY

Matt knocks one more time.

                        MATT

Dedee?

INT. MOTEL ROOM – DAY

Finally, the SOUND OF KNOCKING wakes up Dedee – who suddenly realizes that the body she is sleeping next to is a corpse. She freaks, jumps out of bed, then freezes as she realizes that someone's at the door. She's not going to answer until:

                        MATT (O.S.)
Dedee? Come on, it's me, Matt. Open up.

                        DEDEE
                    (*relieved*)
My God . . .

She flips the quilt over Randy's body, goes to the door, opens it, falls into Matt's arms.

I'm so glad you're here.

                        MATT
Listen, Dedee, I know you don't want to come back to Indiana to have the baby –

                        DEDEE
I do. Indiana, Louisiana, anywhere. Let's go.

                        MATT
You mean now? What about this Randy guy?

                        DEDEE
He's a jerk. I can't stand him. Not that we fight or anything. He's just –

A CAR HORN BEEPS from below.

Who's that?

MATT

Lucia, Bill, and Carl.

DEDEE

Who's Carl?

MATT

This friend of ours. Sheriff from back home. That's how we found you.

DEDEE
(*not liking this*)
Oh. Could I see you inside for just a minute?

INT. MOTEL ROOM — DAY

No sooner are they in the door than Dedee gives Matt a long hard kiss on the mouth. He breaks for air.

MATT

Jesus, Dedee . . .

DEDEE
(*whispering*)
I missed you so much.

MATT

I don't know, Dedee . . .

She keeps kissing him, then whispers in his ear:

DEDEE

Randy's dead.

MATT

What?

Dedee whispers, motions for him to be quiet.

DEDEE

Shhh. He's under the quilt.

Matt uncovers the body.

MATT

Jesus Christ.

Matt feels for a pulse, starts mouth-to-mouth.

DEDEE

For God's sake, Matt, he's dead. Stop it – look at him. He's the color of a sink.

Matt sits back, looks at the body.

It was suicide. It's been coming for years. He shot himself.

MATT

In the back of the head?

DEDEE

He was always very limber, he had that going for him. You believe me, don't you?

MATT

Of course I do. It wasn't his baby, was it?

DEDEE

No.

MATT

And it's not mine.

DEDEE

Not really.

MATT

Then who's –

DEDEE

It's gonna have to be by process of elimination and we just don't have the time for that.

MATT

Dedee, this is going to look really bad.

DEDEE

I got to ask you a question, Matt, and I want you to answer me really honestly. Do you still love me?

MATT

Well, sure, but . . .

DEDEE

And do you love my unborn child even though it's highly unlikely it has anything to do with you?

MATT

Unlikely doesn't mean impossible.

DEDEE

Well, when it comes out, do you want the first thing it sees to be a jail cell?

MATT

Do they see right away?

DEDEE

Matt, the jail part's the thing here. I'll be in jail.

MATT

Oh. Why?

DEDEE

Because people aren't as understanding as you are . . . That's what these past few days have taught me.

Matt nods, trying to keep up.

EXT. MOTEL PARKING LOT — DAY

Lucia has found a rack of Palm Springs brochures and is flipping through them. Bill watches Carl check the parking lot for Randy's car.

LUCIA

I know you think you're being a good guy, but it's really just self-destructive.

BILL

When is it too hot to analyze me? 110 degrees? 115?

LUCIA

You've got a real death wish. It's so selfish. I've got one too, but I direct it towards others.

Behind them two men pull up in a car with PALM SPRINGS HARLEY DAVIDSON *decal'd on the side. Both men get out. One of them carries a helmet; the other goes into the office.*

> (looking at a brochure)
People who believe in outlet stores are the same people who believe in permanent press. Or superglue.

But Bill's watching HARLEY MAN #1 *go up the outside stairs to the second-floor breezeway.*

ON THE BREEZEWAY

Harley Man #1 goes up the stairs to Dedee's room, knocks on Dedee's door.

HARLEY MAN #1
(calling down to Harley Man #2)
No answer. Check the lot in back.

BILL AND LUCIA

Both watching the scene at Dedee's motel door.

BILL

Stay here.

LUCIA

Oh, yeah, of course.

BILL
(calling over to Carl)
Check the back!

Bill heads for the stairs; Lucia's right behind him.

EXT. SECOND-STORY BREEZEWAY — DAY

Bill and Lucia reach Dedee's door. Harley Man #1 is still knocking.

LUCIA

Are you looking for Dedee Truitt?

BILL

Dedee! Matt!

(no answer from within)

Shit!

He stands back, kicks the door with his heel. After a couple of tries, it bursts open.

INT. DEDEE'S MOTEL ROOM — DAY

Empty. Bill and Lucia can hear someone calling to them through the open bathroom window.

CARL (O.S.)
Bill! Are you in?

Bill heads into the bathroom – but Lucia sees what he's missed: Randy's dead body – or rather, Randy's dead foot – peeking out from under the quilt on the bed. She freezes, then approaches the body slowly.

LUCIA
Bill?

She leans over, touches the body – and it starts vibrating from the Magic Fingers. She SCREAMS.

EXT. MOTEL PARKING LOT — DAY

Late afternoon. Police cars, a coroner's wagon, reporters, Harley Man #1 and #2, and all the guests who've been staying at this less-than-Best Western motel fill the parking lot. In the confusion, we find Carl, Lucia, and Bill standing together. Lucia's nervous; Bill's in a funk; Carl's in command.

CARL
They won't get far. They've got an APB out for the motorcycle

LUCIA
All I know is we don't talk without a lawyer. Say nothing. People on *NYPD Blue* only get screwed if they talk.

BILL
That poor kid.

LUCIA
You still think she just needs love? She's a murderer.

                             BILL
We don't know that yet.

                             LUCIA
You better hope she's a murderer. Otherwise Matt is.

A Palm Springs Policewoman, OFFICER JUDY ZALE, comes up to them.

                         OFFICER ZALE
We'd like to ask you to stay in Palm Springs for a few days.

                             LUCIA
Are we under arrest?

                         OFFICER ZALE
                         (*shaking her head*)
At our expense, of course.

                             CARL
You must have a nice budget. Carl Tippett. St. Joe County Sheriff's Department. Indiana.

                         OFFICER ZALE
Oh. Colleague. Actually, we do have a nice little cushion. Not too much crime here. Course we got casinos, drunks, a little drugs. Mostly old people and the gays. Why, you looking for a transfer?

She whispers the words 'the gays', but pleasantly. Lucia eyes this incipient romance sourly, turns to Bill, who's anxiously watching the police radio. It's all too much for her.

                             LUCIA
I'm gonna go check in.

No one responds. She heads off to the motel's office . . .

INT. PALM SPRINGS MOTEL — LUCIA'S ROOM — NIGHT

Lucia is washing out her underwear in the sink with soap. She's been crying. She's pissed off and miserable. There's a bottle of booze in a brown paper bag and half a delivery pizza on the chest of drawers. There's a KNOCK on the door.

LUCIA

I said I'm sleeping!

BILL (O.S.)

Come on, Loosh. Let me in.

Lucia rolls her eyes, opens the door.

LUCIA

Oh good. My delivery from 1-800-Pity.

BILL

We shouldn't be alone. Not after the day we had.

LUCIA

Please. I teach America's youth. I can't be thrown by a vibrating corpse. Any news?

BILL

I was down at the station. They found the motorcycle. Sold it. Probably bought a car. They'll find them.

LUCIA

Then I'll sleep well tonight. Where's Carl?

BILL

I don't know. Bed?

LUCIA

I'll bet.

He helps himself to some pizza. Lucia is trying to hide her wet underwear laundry from Bill. She catches herself.

Like you give a shit. Like this is incendiary material. Like you're the least bit interested.

BILL

What am I supposed to say?

She dangles her bra in front of him.

LUCIA

I could dance around you naked. Vagina, vagina, vagina. Does that word do *anything* for you?

BILL

I don't think it does much for anyone, gay or straight. Too clinical. Like 'dentifrice' for toothpaste.

LUCIA

It's so fucking ironic. You know what my mother said when she found out Tom was gay? 'It's such a lonely life.' She said that to me, the single straight girl. Is that funny or what? I don't know. I just don't get sex.

BILL

You gotta get out more –

LUCIA

No, no, I don't understand sex, I don't get it, get it? It seems like a lot of trouble for not much. Am I the only one who thinks this?

BILL

I don't think you're the tip of an iceberg, frankly.

LUCIA

You get it. Carl gets it. The whole world is sex crazy all of a sudden.

BILL

I think it goes back a little further than that.

LUCIA

I'd rather have a back rub. It lasts longer and there's no, you know, fluids. God, what's so great about that? It's like, 'Hi. I'd like to blow my nose on your face.' You wouldn't like that, would you?

BILL

Yeah, and after they do it, they never phone you.

LUCIA

Or a shampoo. Someone giving you a shampoo, that'd make sense, if you were chasing this asshole all over the country because he gave great shampoos.

BILL

It's not just sex, Lucia. I care about Matt. I used to, anyway.

LUCIA

It's sex, Bill, that's all. You just can't admit it. You want to think you're above it. Nothing that happened happened because you liked sex.

BILL
(*a beat*)
Tom didn't die because of sex.

LUCIA

Didn't he? P.C. crap aside? Didn't sex kill him? I mean, if he just couldn't get enough shampoos or back rubs, wouldn't he be here today?

BILL

I'm really beat –

LUCIA

Sex kills, that's what you can't accept. Why do you think there are no more Hawaiians? You think they'd bother coming up with the phrase 'died in childbirth' if it only happened once? It's fucking dangerous, sex.

BILL

You might as well say I killed him.

LUCIA
(*backing off*)
He didn't get it from you.

BILL

No, he got it from some other faggot, isn't that what you think?

LUCIA

What I think is, fine. Chase this bimbo from Indiana to Chippewa Falls, for all I care. Throw away your reputation, your job, your students – whatever, because you want Matt. You've got the right. Just don't try to tell me it's love, okay? You're an English teacher. Call things by their right name.

It'll be a long time before these two are friends again.

BILL

Okay, fine. Dentifrice. Vagina. And sour fucking grapes. Class dismissed?

He leaves.

EXT. MOTEL BREEZEWAY – NIGHT

Carl has been standing there holding a bag from 7-11. Bill brushes past him, slamming the door. Carl looks at him, decides to say nothing. Waits a moment. Knocks on Lucia's door.

THE DOOR OPENS

. . . and Lucia is there, still furious, thinking it's Bill.

CARL

I heard . . . Anything I can do?

LUCIA

Where's Pepper? Police Woman?

CARL

I don't know. Here. I bought you some beer at the 7-11.
    (*he hands her a bottle of shampoo; sheepishly*)
I needed shampoo. Are you okay?

LUCIA

Headache.

CARL

I give good neck-rubs.

Suddenly, she grabs him, kisses him hard. He drops the grocery bag; we hear beer fizzing out of breaking bottles. Together they stumble back into the room. Carl kicks the door shut, locking us out. We STAY ON THE CLOSED DOOR . . .

DEDEE (V.O.)

Can you believe this? It's so unfair. She spent her whole life being a total pill and this happens to her. We're not going inside. It's too, like, gross. She turned out to be one of those talkers. You know what I mean?

> (*uninflected*)
> Do it to me, yeah, oh there, take me home, oh baby.
> (*back to normal*)
> Sickening. Oh, here she comes.

LATER

The door opens, Lucia comes out, looking flushed and happy . . . She picks through the broken bag, finds the bottle of shampoo. Returns happily inside.

> DEDEE (V.O.)
> Yuck. Meanwhile, I'm like God knows where with Matt, running from the police and trying to get into it . . .

Meanwhile, CAMERA is turning slowly to . . .

EXT. THE PARKING LOT — DAY

Through a TIME DISSOLVE, the parking lot comes to life. Carl and Lucia come downstairs with their suitcases; then Bill. They talk. Bill goes over to his rental car, drives off. Lucia and Carl watch, then get into Carl's car.

> DEDEE (V.O.)
> Believe it or not, we didn't get caught. The police were dumber than us, which wasn't easy 'cause Matt insisted on calling the shots. And you know Matt. If opposites really attract, he'll be getting hosed by Albert Einstein any day now.

EXT. SOUTH BEND — BILL'S HOUSE — DAY

Bill's car is being followed by lots of press. There are even more camped out on his front lawn.

> DEDEE (V.O.)
> It was a bigger story than we figured. Someone in Palm Springs tipped off the local press, and they had a kind of a Welcome Home parade for him.

TV SCREEN

WNN reports on 'SHAME IN THE RUST BELT'.

                              DEDEE (V.O.)
Everything Bill touched was turning to shit. That creep Jason
wasn't withdrawing his charges.

TV SCREEN

Now Jason is being interviewed.

                              JASON
I just don't want this to happen to another kid. If I save one
kid from being (*censored beep*), having his (*censored beep*)
totally (*censored beep*) till he's (*beeped*), then maybe all this has
been worth something. Teachers everywhere have to learn
that no means no. At least until we've dropped out.

                              DEDEE (V.O.)
The school board scheduled a hearing, and the D.A.
launched a probe, so to speak.

KULP HOUSE — BOBETTE'S LIVING ROOM

*Bobette is watching the WNN report. Dedee's picture is in the upper
right-hand corner of the TV screen.*

                              DEDEE (V.O.)
And my mom hired a lawyer in Crevecoeur to try to get
some money from Bill.

EXT. KULP HOUSE, CREVECOEUR — FRONT PORCH — DAY

*An impromptu press conference with a visual aid: a poster-sized blown-
up picture of Dedee which is a trimmed snapshot. Obviously Dedee was
holding a joint – there's a snip taken out of the photo there – and a
drink. She's exhaling and laughing. Bobette appears tearful with her
publicity-hungry ATTORNEY.*

                              DEDEE (V.O.)
Meanwhile, nobody knew where we were.

EXT. BILL'S HOUSE — DAY

*Almost all the windows on the bottom floor and some on the second are
boarded up with cardboard.*

EXT. BILL'S BACKYARD — DAY

The rock garden is taking shape.

EXT. SOUTH BEND CEMETERY — DAY

Bill is sipping some blended whipped coffee drink looking down at a grave. We read the tombstone: 'TOM DALURY. Beloved Companion and Brother. 1962–1994'.

A car door slams. Carl heads up the hill, stops beside Bill.

BILL

You following me? Or am I under arrest?

CARL

Nancy's buried here. Came to pay my respects.
(he looks a moment at Tom's grave)
I thought you had him cremated.

BILL

Half the ashes here, half in the jar. That's the beauty of cremation. Spread the wealth.

CARL

Nice headstone.

BILL

'Beloved companion.' Sounds like I buried my setter. It was Lucia's idea.

CARL
(looking at the plot)
You could use some zinnias.

BILL

Don't go fag on me, man.

CARL

Lucia says hi.

BILL

Hi back.

He tips the rest of his drink over the grave like an offering to the gods.

CARL

I heard you got yourself a lawyer.

BILL

He thinks my union's gonna screw me. I heard from this gay defense fund, though. They want to help – if I take a lie-detector test.

CARL

She really would like to hear from you.

BILL

Message delivered.

CARL

Come on, look at you. You look like shit. Admit it. You miss her.

BILL

Hey, Carl. You've been a good friend. Lucia too. But the one I miss is Matt.

CARL

Oh yeah, sure.

BILL

Still makes you a little queasy, huh? You straight boys never quite get over *Deliverance*.

CARL

Guess we all tighten up a little when we hear a banjo.

BILL

I wish he were perfect. But he's not. He's a screw-up who's too naïve to be really bad with a knack, a fucking rare knack if you want to know the truth, of making me feel good. When he wasn't pissing me off. But not perfect. I'm not saying I miss someone perfect. You get a perfect one?

CARL

Not so's you'd notice.

BILL

Welcome to the club.

CARL

Pleased to be here.

A moment. They both look out over the cemetery. Then:

BILL

Well. You take care.

He heads down to his car. Carl watches him go.

INT. HIGH-SCHOOL CORRIDOR — DAY

Bill carries a box of his belongings through the hallways. He passes Joe, the kid he chastised in the boys' bathroom, who's putting up a WELCOME FRESHMEN *banner. Joe salutes him. Bill nods.*

DEDEE (V.O.)

He didn't even have the hearing. The Jason kid disappeared, so the charges were dropped, but Bill resigned anyway. School started. People forgot about him. Except you-know-who. The stalker.

EXT. BILL'S HOUSE — DAY

A realtor is hammering a FOR SALE *sign into Bill's front lawn. PAN OVER TO SEE Lucia's car. She sees this. She waits till the realtor goes, then hurries to the front door, knocks. No answer. She uses her key — but the locks have been changed.*

DEDEE (V.O.)

Gay houses usually sell really quickly because of the recessed lighting and the good faucets. The realtor said the boarded-up windows were the kind of challenge she liked . . .

EXT. BILL'S HOUSE — DECK — DAY

Bill, wrapped up in an overcoat on the deck, hears the doorbell but doesn't move. Just looks out over the garden.

DEDEE (V.O.)

. . . so it would've ended really differently if we'd waited one or two days more than we did, but we didn't. It was October.

EXT. BILL'S HOUSE – FRONT YARD – DAY

Just before sun-up. A car is idling in front of Bill's house.

INT. BILL'S HOUSE – LIVING ROOM – DAY

Through new glass windows, the masking tape still on them, Bill looks at the tail-lights of the idling car. He picks up a baseball bat, grabs his coat. Under his breath:

BILL
Gimme a break. I'm still in escrow.

He leaves. We SEE NOW that there are packing cartons everywhere.

EXT. BILL'S HOUSE – FRONT LAWN – DAY

Bill heads across the grass to the car. There's an IN ESCROW banner on the realtor's sign. He reaches the beat-up car, taps on the passenger window with the tip of the bat. Someone leans over, winds down the window. It's Jason.

JASON
Hey, man. How's it going?

BILL
Where the hell have you been? We couldn't hold the hearing.

JASON
I was busy.

BILL
Well, fuck you. And good luck re-filing those charges –

JASON
Hey! That's not why I'm here.

He holds up a cassette.

Curious?

He opens the car door. After a moment, Bill gets in.

INT. JASON'S CAR – (STATIONARY) – DAY

Jason pushes the cassette into the player, turns up the volume.

DEDEE'S VOICE

Is this on? Okay. Bill? Bill, this is Dedee, your sister. I had to send Jason because of the crime thing. Matt called him one night in Chicago and he's been like, a fairy godfather so to speak – what? – he wants me to say faggot godfather – and anyway, I'm going to have the baby and we need money and you're the only one I know who has money. Like, $10,000.

Bill looks at Jason, who shrugs.

JASON

We got a little wiggle room there.

DEDEE'S VOICE

Because Matt isn't working too regular and neither am I, and we do have expenses, and if you give us the money – Jason, hold up the envelope now – inside the envelope are these letters where Jason takes back everything, so you'll get your job back. Plus I'll send you pictures of the baby when it comes out, because it will be your niece or nephew . . . Okay, turn it off. Oh, also Matt says hi.

The tape ends. Jason turns off the player, dangles the envelope in front of Bill.

JASON

So, what do you think?

BILL

Where are they?

JASON

Can't tell you. You just give me the money and that's it.

Bill looks at him, looks as if he's going to agree. But instead he grabs Jason's pierced nipple through his undershirt and twists it. Jason yelps.

Hey, that's pierced!

BILL

Listen to me, you little grunge faggot. I've survived my family, my schoolyard, every Republican, every other Democrat, Anita Bryant, the Pope, the Fucking Christian Coalition, not to mention a real sonofabitch of a virus, in case you haven't noticed, and all that time, since Paul Lynde and Truman Capote were the only fairies in America, I was busting my ass so you could do what you want with yours, so I don't just want your obedience, which I do want, and plenty of it, but I want your fucking gratitude right fucking now, or you'll be looking down a long road at your nipple on the ground, you know what I'm saying? *Take me to them.*

JASON

Jesus. All right. Come on, let go.

Bill lets him go. Jason brushes the tears from his eyes. Man, that hurt.

You're supposed to be my brother, man.

BILL

Hey, I *was* brotherly, man. Think where else you're pierced. Come on. Move it.

Jason covers his groin with his free hand, pulls out.

EXT. LUCIA'S HOUSE – DAY

Lucia gets into her car, ready for work. She puts her coffee mug on top of the car while she unlocks her door; it falls off, smashes. She wanted that coffee.

EXT. CONVENIENCE STORE – DAY

Lucia pulls into the parking lot next to Randy's car. She doesn't see Bill inside the car, playing and replaying the tape. He doesn't see her.

INT. CONVENIENCE STORE – DAY

Jason's at the register buying an armful of junk food.

JASON

Oh, man, teriyaki. They just have regular Slim Jims in Canada.

Lucia, getting herself some coffee, sees him, recognizes him.

LUCIA

Jason? Jason Bock?

CASHIER
Oh my God, yeah. The gay.

JASON
Uh, hey, Ms. Dalury. How you doing?

LUCIA
Never mind about me. I hope you're in town to clear Mr. Truitt's name.

JASON
Oh, he never did anything to me, Ms. Dalury. That was just leverage.

LUCIA
Lever – you're going to march right into school with me, young man, and make a statement to the principal, and then we're going to the police and Detective Tippett will –

JASON
I'm just passing through, ma'am.

LUCIA
You owe him that much!

JASON
Sorry.

He hastily grabs his bag of junk food and leaves.

LUCIA
I should have flunked you when I had the chance!

She turns to look at the cashier, a young girl she also taught.

CASHIER
His skin cleared up though.

INT./EXT. JASON'S CAR – PARKING LOT – DAY

Jason jumps in, hands Bill his coffee, starts the car quickly.

BILL
You paid, didn't you? You didn't –

                    JASON
Fucking small town, man . . .

INT. CONVENIENCE STORE — DAY

Lucia watches Jason's car pull out, trying to read the license plate. She freezes as she gets a glimpse of Jason's passenger. Bill doesn't see her. A moment, then she turns to the cashier.

                    LUCIA
Call the school, tell 'em I'm sick.
          (*as the girl hesitates*)
Do it!

And Lucia runs to her car, dumping her coffee as she goes.

SERIES OF SHOTS — THE PURSUIT

Jason's car, followed discreetly by Lucia's Explorer, heads east out of South Bend and then north into Michigan, towards and through Detroit, crossing into Canada, heading towards Toronto.

It's after noon when Jason's car finally turns down a country road thirty miles from Toronto.

EXT. CANADIAN COUNTRY ROAD — DAY

Jason's driving down this dirt road.

                    JASON
As soon as the baby's born, we go to Mexico. Me, Matt, and the kid.
          (*off Bill's look*)
Dedee knows she's not the mommy type. So, you know . . . the baby's available.

                    BILL
Matt's not straight anymore?

                    JASON
Hey, he called me, didn't he?

                    BILL
Yeah, he did.

The road dead-ends in front of a two-story summer cabin.

JASON

We got it cheap because of the season.

BILL

Send Matt out first.

JASON

Boy. She's gonna kill me when she sees you. Don't tell her you don't have the money till later, okay?

Off Bill's look, he gets out of the car, heads into the house. Bill gets out to stretch his legs. He starts coming closer to the house when he hears:

DEDEE (O.S.)

What the hell are you doing here?

He turns around to see Dedee, eight-and-a-half months pregnant, carrying a bundle of kindling she's been gathering.

BILL

Jesus, Dedee – God, you're huge.

DEDEE

Jason!

Jason pops his head out of the front door of the cabin.

JASON

Oh, hey Deed. We're back. He wanted to see you himself. Family, you know.

DEDEE

Asshole! Go in and help Matt get dinner. I'll handle him.

Jason nods, goes back inside the cabin.

BILL

You'll handle me? Did you really think I'd just load up his car with cash and point it north?

DEDEE

You're screwing it all up.

BILL

When are you due? What's the doctor say?

DEDEE

We can't afford a doctor – didn't you listen to the tape?

BILL

Come on, you're coming home with me –

DEDEE

You didn't bring any money at all?

BILL
(*sitting down*)

Forget the money.

DEDEE

It's not for me – it's for them. Part of it, anyway. Did he tell you they're going to Mexico?

BILL

And you're giving them the baby as some kind of a wedding gift? 'Cause who needs another blender, right?

DEDEE

I gotta get Matt's name on the certificate. They'll take my word for it, right? Once he's the father he can take the kid anywhere.

BILL

Just give it away?

DEDEE

It's his just as much as mine. At least that's the line I'm going to take.

BILL

Dedee, come on. You can't live like this. It's crazy. If you want to give up your baby, there are agencies. You got to be reasonable. Besides . . . you're wanted for murder back home.

DEDEE

For questioning. I don't want to talk about it.

BILL

I could turn you over to the police right now. Not could, should.

DEDEE

I'm your sister, okay? God. Plus I made Jason take back everything he said in those letters. They'll get the cops off your back. Thanks to me.

From behind them:

MATT (O.S.)

Hey, Bill!

Bill turns, sees . . .

BILL'S POV — MATT

Matt is at the doorway of the cabin. His face is flushed; his shirt unbuttoned. He slaps away the hands of a barely seen Jason behind him, then he waves Bill inside.

MATT

Hungry?

BACK TO BILL AND DEDEE

Dedee turns to Bill, shrugs.

DEDEE

It's the life cycle of the American bisexual. He's in the last stage. Total 'mo.

EXT. CABIN — NIGHT

Having parked her Explorer, Lucia creeps forward slowly, circles the cabin.

HER POV — CABIN

Inside, Dedee, Matt, Jason, and Bill are finishing dinner. Matt and Jason are having words.

BACK TO LUCIA

She's starving, her mouth watering. Then she stumbles, hides quickly as:

EXT. CABIN — PORCH — NIGHT

Bill and Matt come out with their coffee.

MATT

He's such a jerk sometimes.

BILL

He's always been nice to me, you know. In between filing charges.

MATT

That's what I mean. Jerk.

BILL
(*hopeful*)
Sounds like a volatile relationship.

MATT

Yeah. You mean, like, in bed it doesn't matter who's on top?

BILL

That's versatile. Volatile means you fight a lot.

MATT

All the time.

BILL

Think that'll be good for the kid?

MATT

Everyone fights.
(*a suspicion*)
Oh. You don't believe in gay parents.

BILL

It's not politics, Matt. It's a kid's life.

MATT
(*about to go inside*)
You know what? Good night.

Bill touches his arm.

BILL

Hey. Hey. Come on. What are you angry about?

MATT

You piss me off. You always did.

BILL

No, I didn't. You were never pissed off.

MATT
If you say so.

BILL
I should be pissed off! You leave me in Palm Springs with the police and the body of that poor kid –

MATT
It was an accident. They were struggling and the gun went off. It's made her very anti-handgun.

BILL
– you disappear for months, months. Not a word. Nothing to let me know you were alive.

MATT
Sorry.

BILL
Course, I don't know why I'm surprised. It's not like I could expect, you know, loyalty or consideration or whatever from you.

MATT
Hey, I told you, I didn't sleep with Jason when I was with you. I just cheated with Dedee there at the end.

BILL
Oh. Well, phew.

MATT
I know it was wrong. But I wasn't happy, Bill. I'm happy with Jason.

BILL
How? I mean . . . he's not on your level, you know.

MATT
I know that's what Lucia used to say about me.

BILL
Ah, come on, Matt, admit it. This thing between you and Jason is just sex –

MATT
– yeah, and that stuff you're breathing is just oxygen –

BILL
It's just an itch. You scratch it, you feel better.

MATT
A lot better.

BILL
Take off your shirt.
           (*off Matt's look*)
Experiment. Take it off. I'm not going to touch you.

Matt unbuttons his shirt, opens it so Bill can see his chest.

MATT
What'd you do with the Polaroids?

BILL
Look at you.

He turns him to face the window. Matt can see his reflection in it.

It's a body, that's all. There's nothing personal about it, there's nothing Matt about it. You don't even work out for it. It's just a package. It hides what's inside, what's really personal. That's what I wanted.

MATT
I don't think I get more personal than my own nipples.

He buttons up his shirt, puts some distance between them.

BILL
There's more to you than that.

MATT
Yeah, but there's at least that. Look, Bill. You think too much. You wanted me. I was fine with that – to me it was flattering. I'm stupid enough I took it personally. But it wasn't enough for you. You had to like make it bigger or something. Make it spiritual or mental or something, like that's some kind of promotion.

BILL

Oh. So there's nothing more to you than the body?

MATT

What the fuck do I know? I'm just saying, if you say you're in love with my mind, hey, I know that's not my best feature. So where does that leave me? Not only does my boyfriend have a fool for a lover, so do I.

BILL

You're not a fool.

MATT

You know what I'm not? Tom.

BILL
(*utterly thrown*)

Tom?

MATT

Sorry he's dead. I don't know much about heaven or stuff. But wherever he is, I don't think he cares that we screwed around. Or feels better because you moved me in and told everyone it was more than sex. He died and it really sucked and you don't get to make it better by living a certain way and being this great guy who likes the insides of people. He was still robbed, and you were too. Even Lucia, who I could care less about.

BILL

Couldn't care less. Sorry.

MATT

Maybe Jason can drive you back tomorrow.

BILL

Maybe so.

MATT

Okay. Good night. You look cute, kind of all stupid-like.

He leans in, kisses Bill lightly on the mouth. Bill kisses him back, not so lightly. Matt smiles, goes into the house.

> DEDEE (V.O.)
> Can I just say to all the girls out there, if you're sitting next to a guy who groaned or made some crack during that little kiss, you're with what we call a closet case. That's the number one tip-off. Number two is if they freak out about gays in the military. You know, if they can't discuss it without giggling about showering with gays and bending over for soap and shit . . . That's not good. Real straight men don't spend a whole lot of time imagining other men naked, if you ask me.

Bill sinks down, sits on the top step, rests his head on his arms. Then he hears someone sniffling. He goes to the end of the porch and sees Lucia. He's stunned.

> BILL
> Lucia? What – ?

Lucia looks up. She's been crying. She dries up quick.

> LUCIA
> Oh, God. I'm sorry. It was that stuff about Tom.

> BILL
> How'd you get here?

> LUCIA
> I followed you guys from the 7-11. Do you have anything to eat?

INT. KITCHEN – NIGHT

Everyone is upstairs. Lucia wolfs down some food.

> LUCIA
> I kept thinking you were gonna pull over and I could, you know, jump out and protect you.

> BILL
> I wasn't too protected.

> LUCIA
> So I heard. What do we do now?

> BILL
> I'm gonna stay for a couple days. See if I can convince her to

have the baby in the States. Drag Jason back to make a statement to the board. Like I give a shit.

She starts crying again.

What? Come on, stop that.

He has to go over, sit down beside her, put his arm around her.

LUCIA
Are you just never going to call me again?

BILL
I don't need to. You can just keep tailing me.

LUCIA
Matt thinks it was just sex too, so I'm not completely off.

BILL
Yeah, but he has a higher opinion of sex than you do.

LUCIA
You mean used to.

BILL
Congratulations.

LUCIA
Congratulate Carl. I'm not gonna say I'm sorry. Because I did already in that letter you didn't read.

BILL
I read it. I'm sorry too – about the sour grapes thing. Are you gonna stay the night? We got beds.

LUCIA
(*shaking her head*)
I'm gonna head back. Can I call Carl? I just want to tell him everything's okay. I mean, it is okay, isn't it?

BILL
Yeah, Lucia. It's okay.

Suddenly, THEY HEAR A SCREAM from upstairs. Bill and Lucia look at each other, then run –

INT. CABIN – SECOND FLOOR – NIGHT

Bill and Lucia run upstairs. They see Jason in the hallway.

> JASON
> Jesus! Oh, Ms. Dalury – what are you –
>
> LUCIA
> Never mind. Call 911 – do they have 911 here?

They run into:

INT. DEDEE'S BEDROOM – NIGHT

Dedee is scared now. There's blood on the sheets. She's sweating and nervous. Matt's with her.

> DEDEE
> Shit, shit, shit . . .
>
> MATT
> It's okay, it's okay, we're getting a doctor –
>
> DEDEE
> What the fuck is she doing here?
>
> MATT
> Lucia?
>
> LUCIA
> Go help Jason – find out how fast they can get an ambulance here. What happened?
>
> DEDEE
> I don't know. I was asleep. Look at the blood –
>
> LUCIA
> You're not hemorrhaging, okay? Are you having contractions?
>
> DEDEE
> No, this is my sleepy face, what the fuck do you think?
>
> BILL
> *(yelling out the door)*
> Matt – what's going on?

                    MATT (O.S.)
We can't reach them.

                    BILL
Do you know where the hospital is?

                    DEDEE
Yeah. I had bleeding once before.

                    BILL
We'll take Jason's car.

                    LUCIA
Mine's bigger.

EXT. CABIN — NIGHT

Bill is carrying Dedee out to the car; Matt's running next to her with a bag. Jason's behind the wheel of his car; Lucia's behind hers, the motor running, the lights on. Matt opens the hatchback of Lucia's car. They put Dedee in gently. Matt starts to crawl in after her.

                    DEDEE
Bill.

Bill nods, crawls in beside her. Matt closes the hatchback. Jason yells out his window:

                    JASON
Do they have credit cards? They won't take her without money!

Matt runs over to Jason's car.

                    MATT
Yeah, it's cool. Let's go.
                    (*calling back to Lucia*)
Follow us!

The two cars pull off.

INT. LUCIA'S EXPLORER — BACK — (MOVING) — NIGHT

Bill and Dedee together. Dedee winces when the car hits a pothole.

LUCIA

Sorry!

BILL

You okay?

Dedee, in too much pain to be smart, nods, takes his hand when he offers it.

EXT. COUNTRY ROAD — NIGHT

The two cars barrel down the road. Another car comes toward them.

INT. LUCIA'S CAR — (MOVING) — NIGHT

Lucia sees the lights of the other car approaching.

LUCIA

Is that the ambulance?

The car passes them.

LUCIA'S POV — THE OTHER DRIVER

. . . is Carl. He looks almost as surprised as they are.

BACK TO SCENE

Lucia is shocked; so is Bill, who's seen it too.

LUCIA

How the hell . . .

BILL

Keep driving.

Behind her we see (in reverse) the decal for 'Lo-Jack Automobile Theft Tracking System' . . .

EXT. CANADIAN ROAD — NIGHT

Carl's car makes a three-point turn, starts to follow Lucia and Jason's car. A Canadian police car, cherries spinning, begins to pursue them.

EXT. CANADIAN HOSPITAL – NIGHT

First Jason, then Lucia, then Carl, then the Canadian police car pull up into Emergency. Everyone gets out of their cars in the off-loading zone, over the protests of the Emergency Room staff.

LUCIA
What the hell are you doing here?!

BILL
Excuse me.

He gets a wheelchair. Lucia comes around from the front of the car.

LUCIA
Why are you following me?

MATT
Is there a doctor here? Excuse me? Are you a doctor?

Carl sees Jason. His eyes pop.

CARL
You little shit –

JASON
Be cool, man. We're in Canada.

Bill helps Dedee out of the car into the wheelchair.

LUCIA
Matt – go tell them inside.

CARL
What's going on?

DEDEE
Bring my bag!

LUCIA
(*to Carl*)
Handle your friends for me, honey, okay?

Everyone except Carl rushes into the Emergency Room.

INT. EMERGENCY ROOM — NURSES' STATION — NIGHT

Lucia, Matt, Jason, Bill, Dedee – and NURSE TAMMY BING filling out a form.

NURSE BING
Dedee Truitt. Is the father here?

MATT
Probably.

DEDEE
Matt!

MATT
Yes. I am. I'm the father.

JASON
I'm the father's boyfriend.

Dedee moans, and a few drops of blood hit the floor. Jason looks at it and falters, about to faint. Bill notices.

BILL
Matt?

MATT
Shit! Jason!

BILL
Go ahead, go ahead, take care of him.
      (off the nurse's look)
I'm her brother.

NURSE BING
And you?

BILL
She's family.

LUCIA
I'm Tom's sister.

NURSE BING
Who's Tom?

                    LUCIA

He's my brother –

                    JASON

Don't worry, he's dead.

                    DEDEE

Hey, what do I have to do? Bleed from the eyes? Come on, deliver me!

                    NURSE BING

We have a procedure here . . .

Suddenly Dedee starts screaming – a loud, impressive wail, and Nurse Bing drops her clipboard, shouts out a code blue! Everyone's astonished.

                    MATT

That sounds like it really smarts.

                    BILL

Where do I take her?

                    NURSE BING
                    (*to an orderly*)

George! Four.

George begins to wheel off Dedee. Lucia, Matt, Jason, and Bill start to follow.

Only one of you goes with her!

                    BILL

Dedee?

Dedee looks up at Bill, nods. Bill turns to the others.

I'll let you know.

INT. EMERGENCY ROOM – NIGHT

A young DOCTOR ALLEN looks at Dedee.

                    DOCTOR ALLEN

Jesus, it's crowning.

DEDEE

What does that mean?

BILL

He can see the head.

DEDEE

Duh. It's huge. He could see it from space.

BILL

Aren't you supposed to be breathing?

DEDEE

Oh, that's better. It's over. Jesus.

BILL

Is this normal?

DOCTOR ALLEN

Yeah, sure, sure.

He looks nervous. As he and the nurses confer...

BILL

Wow. You're having a baby.

DEDEE

Yeah. Lucky me.

BILL

Uncle Bill.

DEDEE

Dad's first grandchild.

BILL

Wow.

DEDEE

I don't remember much about him.

BILL

You were five.

DEDEE

He liked these shirts. Made of like nylon or something – you know the kind I mean?

BILL

Ban-Lon. He was the Ban-Lon king.

DEDEE

They didn't breathe, you know. He'd mow the lawn in them and really stink. Not much to hold on to. He wore plastic and stank.

BILL

We'll call your mom if you want after this.

DEDEE

No. Bill . . .

BILL

Is another one coming?

DEDEE

Where's my bag?

BILL

Lucia has it. You need something?

DEDEE

The ashes are in there. Tom's. And every single bit of him's there. I double-bagged it.

BILL

Oh. Good.

DEDEE

It was pretty fucking low. Just so you know I know. I wouldn't want that on my conscience. Like I have one.

BILL

You don't have to tell me that now, okay? Everything's gonna be fine.

DEDEE

It's Randy's baby. Randy –

She starts panting now, feeling the contraction coming.

BILL

I know it was an accident. You don't have to tell me anything. Everything's going to be fine.

DEDEE

I don't want you to think I'm never thinking about Randy.

BILL

I don't think that. Shhh.

DEDEE

One more thing. If something happens to me, I want you to have the baby. Not them. You'll be the uncle.

BILL

Nothing's going to happen to you.

The contraction arrives. Dedee looks at Bill, panic in her eyes. He holds on to her.

DEDEE (V.O.)

Excuse me, but haven't we seen this scene like a million times before? I pant and swear and I'm like, you know, pissed off, women delivering are always pissed off and asking for that shot, that epidural or whatever, and swearing at the man who got them into it, etc., and the husband's holding the video camera – we don't have one here, but other than that it's pretty standard. So I gotta give you something else to watch and you feel free to go back and forth.

SPLIT SCREEN:

DEDEE'S DELIVERY AND –
EXT. EMERGENCY ROOM SMOKING WAITING AREA – NIGHT

Lucia comes out to find Carl getting a drink from a vending machine. He sees her.

CARL

Want one?

Lucia shakes her head. The atmosphere is strained.

LUCIA

I'm sorry, okay? There wasn't time to pull over.

CARL

What's the point, Lucia?

LUCIA

The point of what?

CARL

What's the point of sleeping with you if it doesn't get your attention? If I always come second to Bill?

LUCIA

Excuse me?

CARL

Say the point of sex isn't recreation or procreation or any of that stuff. Say it's concentration. Say it's supposed to focus your attention on the person you're sleeping with. Like biological highlighter. Otherwise, there's just too many people in the world.

LUCIA

Just because I sleep with you, I don't care about anyone else?

CARL

Look for me first in any crowded room. Yeah. And I do likewise.

LUCIA

This rule's written down somewhere?

CARL

Otherwise I find someone else to sleep with.

1 beat.

LUCIA

It's a habit, thinking of Bill. Because of Tom.

CARL

I know.

LUCIA
So if you come first –

CARL
And you come first with me –

LUCIA
Where does the kid come?

CARL
What kid?

LUCIA
Maybe you better leave all that shit about the purpose of sex to someone more qualified.

CARL
You're pregnant?

LUCIA
And let me tell you something, honey. It ain't Bill's.

He grabs her, kisses her . . .

SPLIT SCREEN ENDS

INT. EMERGENCY ROOM – NIGHT

During the previous scene, Dedee's labor has progressed. Now the baby's being born.

DOCTOR
It's a boy!

Dedee collapses on the pillows. Bill leans in to her.

BILL
He's beautiful, Dedee. He's a beautiful boy.

DEDEE
Yeah? Do me a favor.
              (*her eyes close*)
Count his balls.

Bill smiles – but he doesn't like the look on Dedee's face. She's white. Suddenly, he hears a SPLASHING SOUND.

QUICK CUT

Blood is spilling onto the tile floor. Dedee's hemorrhaging.

BACK TO SCENE

> BILL

Doctor!

But the team is already on it. Controlled urgency . . . Bill is shoved to one side . . .

Dedee! Dedee!

But she is white, still . . .

INT. EMERGENCY WAITING ROOM — NIGHT (M.O.S.)

Lucia, Carl, Jason, Matt look up as Bill comes in from the examining room. His clothes are covered with blood.

He looks lost. Lucia stands, goes to him. Matt asks him what happened; Jason pulls Matt's head onto his shoulder.

> DEDEE (V.O.)
> What a bummer. Didn't think I could die, did you? Look at them. Who'd'a thought they gave a shit? Even the bitch, look at her. Unless she's crying for Bill, not me. Contact grief. No, I think it's for me. Look at Bill. I did nothing but fuck up his life. I knew Matt liked me. Look at Jason. He's got a boner, believe it or not. Drama queen. And like these guys, some of you guys ended up liking me. Thought maybe, just maybe I wasn't a total shit.
> *(beat)*
> But you were wrong. I'm fucking with you right now. No way I died. I could have, that much is true. The river of blood thing, that happened. But they stopped it.

INT. EMERGENCY ROOM — EXAMINING ROOM — NIGHT

The doctors stop the flow of blood. Bill fights his way back to Dedee's side. Her eyes flicker open. She sees Bill, smiles, closes her eyes again.

INT. EMERGENCY ROOM — WAITING AREA — NIGHT

As before, except Bill comes in bloody but smiling.

BILL

Baby boy.

Jason and Matt slap hands.

Ten pounds, two ounces.

LUCIA

Yeah, it's yours, Matt. That's a preemie all right.

Amid the general rejoicing, Bill has gone over to Dedee's bag. He is looking inside at the unseen ashes. He puts his hands over his face. Carl comes over to him. Puts an arm on his shoulder.

CARL

You okay, buddy?

BILL

Fine. Yeah. Long year.

He catches Lucia's eye. A beat, then:

                    JASON
I'm glad she didn't die and all but, man. She's what I call a
real user.

INT. CANADIAN HOSPITAL ROOM — DAY

Dedee is holding her baby, trying not to like it. Matt and Jason gather around her, cooing over the baby. We PULL BACK TO SHOW two Canadian policemen outside Dedee's hospital-room door.

                    DEDEE (V.O.)
I don't know what's so great about motherhood. Just looking
at that soft spot made me want to scream. I told Matt and
Jason I wanted to keep him, and they were pretty cool about it.
When you nearly hemorrhage to death, people cut you a break.

EXT. HOSPITAL PARKING LOT — NIGHT

Lucia joins Carl by their cars. Embraces him. They watch two Canadian policemen escort Matt to a police car. Jason flips them off (making sure they can't see him).

                    DEDEE (V.O.)
Most of them, anyway.

INT. HOSPITAL ROOM — NIGHT

Bill stares out the window, the baby asleep in his arms. Dedee looks at him. She's struggling with a breast pump.

                    DEDEE (V.O.)
So everybody ended up happy except me and Bill. Which is
probably genetic from our loser dad who spent his life chasing his dick and ended up basically sitting around holding it,
'cause no one else would.

EXT. POLICE CARS CONVOY INTO U.S. FROM CANADA — DAY

Dedee's in one car; Matt's in another; Lucia, Jason, and Carl follow in their cars . . .

                    DEDEE (V.O.)
Carl gets us to return to the States, so he's like, Super Cop.

Matt and I have to go out to Palm Springs and answer all these questions about Randy. Matt gets off scot-free.

INT. JAIL CELL — DAY

Dedee, in a prison jumpsuit, opening a package from Lucia — books on Getting Your High School Degree at Home.

DEDEE (V.O.)
Me, they put in jail for six months for leaving the scene of a crime or something, even though they agreed it wasn't murder or they couldn't prove it. Especially since Randy had left these really crazy writings in the room about Satan and stuff, so that looked good for me. I left the baby with Bill, and he worked it so my probation time was spent at his place in Indiana. Breaking escrow cost him a shitload.

EXT. HOOVER HIGH SCHOOL — FRONT — DAY

Bill drives up; there's a sign over the front door: WELCOME BACK MR. TRUITT.

DEDEE (V.O.)
Jason made this statement that he'd been paid to make his charges by the Christian Right guys on the school board, the ones against evolution and Huck Finn, which was a total lie but even so *they* won't be back for another term. Plus all these gay legal people came down from Chicago and made this huge stink, and the school board begged Bill to come back to work . . .

EXT. BILL'S BACKYARD — DAY

Baby party. Dedee grimaces as she looks in the crib. Matt and Jason, Bill and Randy Jr. are among the guests.

DEDEE (V.O.)
Lucia and Carl had their baby. You can imagine the pick of that litter. It was the kind of kid if you played with it too much after a feeding, *you* threw up. But they loved it. Even the bitch on the Shopping Network sent a gift.

Lucia opens a gift box. It's a Scarlett O'Hara doll whose hoop skirt conceals an extra roll of toilet paper.

TIME CUT TO:

EXT. BILL'S HOUSE — BACKYARD — DAY

The same backyard hours later. Bill's tidying up, keeping an eye on a toddling baby Randy. Dedee is watching him.

DEDEE (V.O.)
Bill was cute with R.J. – that's Randy Jr. – even though it kind of spooked me at first, him changing a boy baby and getting good peeks at his little thing. But he said straight dads change girl babies all the time and nothing ever comes of that. Is he naïve or what? Anyway, R.J. was crazy about him and vice versa, but he never really took to me. Which was fine with me but a little dull. I mean, I'm supposed to hang here with my brother until I'm eighteen. Just the three of us. With once-a-week visits from an officer of the court.

Dedee's PAROLE OFFICER comes out from the house carrying a briefcase. Dedee gives him a sour smile. He goes to Bill, who turns and gives the guy (who's cute) a big, open-mouthed kiss.

It wasn't once-a-week for long.

INT. DEDEE'S BEDROOM — DAY

Dedee packs, checks herself in the mirror, scribbles a note.

We follow her into:

INT. HALLWAY/STAIRS — DAY

She goes past Bill's half-open door and down the stairway. Inside, Bill is watching the Probation Officer playing with Randy Jr. She takes a picture of Bill and R.J. off the wall, tucks it under her arm, sticks the note on the empty nail.

DEDEE (V.O.)
I didn't mind. If there have to be gay people, at least it's nice there are enough of them to go around.

EXT. BILL'S STREET — DAY

Dedee begins walking down the street, turning TO CAMERA occasionally as she hopes for a hitch.

> DEDEE (V.O.)
> Seems like everybody's having sex but me. Good for them. It's not that I'm against sex. I mean, it was clever of God or evolution or whatever to hook the survival of the species to it. Because we're gonna screw around no matter what. It was a smarter thing to pick than, say, the instinct to share your toys or return phone calls. We'd've died out like eons ago.

No cars stop to pick her up. She stops, sighs, lights a cigarette. AS WE DOLLY CLOSER ...

> But on the minus side ... God. All the attachment that goes with it. It's like this net. Sex always ends in kids or diseases or like, you know. Relationships. That's exactly what I don't want. I want the opposite of all that, whatever that is. Because it's not worth it, not really, is it?

MONTAGE

A MONTAGE of all the moments of physical affection we've seen, and some we haven't. Matt and Bill hugging; Matt and Jason at the cabin; Bill, Lucia, and Tom watching TV on the couch; Lucia hugging Tom when he gives her the house; Bill and Tom in bed, Tom sleeping, Bill feeling his forehead for fever; Lucia and Carl kissing; Lucia with her baby.

And finally, a moment that happened months before we met any of these people: a younger, happier Dedee kissing Randy at sunset in Louisiana ...

END OF MONTAGE

EXT. STREET — DEDEE — DAY

Dedee frowns.

> DEDEE (V.O.)
> Okay, so maybe I'm wrong. Maybe it's not all shit. Maybe – goddammit!

(*she sits down on the curb*)
I thought the whole idea was I know what happens next. I'll tell you one thing, I'm not gonna go back to Bill's house and be this big changed person for you. I told you right off, I don't grow a heart of gold. And if I do, which is like, so unlikely – give me a break and don't make me do it in front of you. Come on, guys, go, okay?
(*directly TO CAMERA*)
Go!

CUT TO BLACK.

A moment, and then:

DEDEE (V.O.)
I'll give you this much, though. 'I never was the same again after that summer.'

FADE OUT.